Rosemarie Allen

D0063014

AMERICAN PROTESTANT WOMEN IN WORLD MISSION

History of the First Feminist Movement in North America

by

R. PIERCE BEAVER

WILLIAM B. EERDMANS PUBLISHING COMPANY
GRAND RAPIDS, MICHIGAN

Library of Congress Cataloging in Publication Data:

Beaver, Robert Pierce, 1906-
   American Protestant women in world mission.

   First ed. (1968) published under title: All
loves excelling.
   Includes indexes.
   1. Women in missionary work.   2. Women
missionaries.   3. Missions, American.
   4. Protestant churches — Missions.   I. Title.
BV2610. B4   1980   266'.023'73   80-14366
ISBN 0-8028-1846-3

To

my mother

CAROLINE NUESCH BEAVER

in honor of

*her lifelong devotion to Christ in
the women's societies of his church*

TABLE OF CONTENTS

PREFACE

FOREIGN MISSIONS WAS THE CONCERN WHICH FOR MORE THAN a century called forth the utmost devotion and effort among American Protestant women. It was for them the grand passion "all loves excelling." Here is the font of all organized women's activities in the churches and to some extent in the community. Out of the inspiration and power generated by the overseas mission there later came separate organization for home missions. That development urgently needs a study parallel to this one for an understanding of the total missionary commitment of Protestant women. It cannot be done here, but the reader should remember that there was this second focus of missionary concern, and that home and foreign missions constantly interacted. No other form of American intervention overseas has made a more powerful cultural impact than this work for women and children. The first necessity in dealing with this colossal enterprise is a description of it in terms of the structures and institutions through which it developed. That is what this book attempts to do. This narrative needs to be supplemented by biographical works, by studies of women's work in the several fields and emerging young churches, and by investigation of women's involvement at the home base.

The author is grateful to the staff of the Missionary Research Library for generous assistance, and likewise to the librarians of Yale University Divinity School Library and of the Congregational Library in Boston. A large number of persons were interviewed, and I express my thanks for the knowledge and insight they shared with me. Miss Margaret T. Applegarth's recollections were helpful. Miss Helen Gallivan made available to me the highly important files of the World's Missionary Committee of Christian Women, the Interdenominational Conference of Woman's Foreign Missionary Societies and its successor Federation, the Com-

mittee on Women's Work, and the Committee on Special
Program and Funds, all in the offices of the Division of
Overseas Ministries of the National Council of Churches.
The entire manuscript was read by Miss Sue Weddell, Miss
Dorothy McConnell, and Ms. Jean Miller, and the helpfulness of their comments and criticisms is gratefully acknowledged. Likewise Dr. Margaret Shannon, Miss Helen Uhrich,
and Mrs. Elizabeth Kinnear read parts of the manuscript and
made valuable suggestions and raised critical issues.

R. P. B.

PREFACE TO THE REVISED EDITION

THE PUBLISHER AND AUTHOR HAVE RECEIVED MANY REQUESTS for the republication of this book, first issued in 1968 under the title *All Loves Excelling: American Protestant Women in World Mission.* The Women's Foreign Mission Movement was the great cause to which American churchwomen were devoted for a century and a half, and it had even more revolutionary impact in Asia and Africa than in the United States and Canada. It began as the first feminist movement in North America and stimulated the rise of various other streams in the nineteenth-century struggle for women's rights and freedom. Now after its decline it is no longer a great creative force within society at large, but it still has impact within the churches, and the forces it set in motion still work for the liberation of women in Asia and Africa. The present struggle for women's full rights in the churches, focusing on ordination and parity in pastoral appointments, has probably deflected from churchwomen's interest in world mission. Yet that mission remains a tremendous challenge to American women. To take into account the recent trends, a final section on the decade of the 1970s has been added.

R. P. B.

I

"FEMALES" BRING THEIR MITES

ONE EVENING IN THE YEAR 1802 SOME GUESTS WERE DINING AT
the table of Deacon John Simpkins and his wife Mehitable
in Boston. A guest raised his wine glass, admired the color
and bouquet of the beverage, and exclaimed: "This excellent wine probably costs a penny a glass. Just think! If we
would each forgo one glass tonight the sum saved would buy
several gospels or more tracts. Should we and our friends
do without some little thing each week and save a cent,
think of the hundreds of Bibles and hymnbooks with which
missionaries could be supplied in just one year's time!"
Evidently dinner conversation had been about missions. The
Deacon was treasurer of the Massachusetts Missionary Society.
Then and there was born the idea of the Cent Society. Mrs.
Simpkins agreed to be the collector, and she would transmit
the collections to her husband for the use of the Society
of which he was treasurer.

Women were already giving their pennies for missions, and
the Cent Society brought forth a flood of copper coins. The

immediate appeal of the new proposal probably lay in the fact that one cent a week was about the sum almost any woman might be able to give if she denied herself some little thing. It appealed also to the widow's two mites of Jesus' parable, and the vision of the collective purchasing power of thousands of pennies made each single cent seem significant. It caught the feminine imagination; Mrs. Simpkins was deluged by pennies.

Ladies had already been organized in support of missions for the past two years. It is not an exaggeration to assert that the hundreds of thousands of later local women's missionary societies, aid societies, and guilds, on the one hand, and the national denominational and interdenominational women's societies, on the other, all find their origin in the heart, mind, will, prayer, and action of an invalid who went about Boston in her "green baize chair." After she had enlisted the interests of friends, Miss Mary Webb gathered together on October 9, 1800, fourteen Baptist and Congregational women, who that afternoon organized the Boston Female Society for Missionary Purposes.[1] The ladies declared themselves animated by the success of contemporary efforts to spread the light of divine truth in many parts of the world and the evident blessing of God on these efforts. Desiring to promote this glorious cause, they would now band together to gather an annual collection to support the work. The annual dues would be two dollars. Their prime motive was that which was then dominant in missions, the giving of glory to God; and the second was "benevolence" and bringing the richest blessings to fellow men. The Society would consist of "females who are disposed to contribute their mite towards so noble a design as diffusion of the gospel light among the shades of darkness and superstition."

---

[1] *A Brief Account of the Origin and Progress of the Boston Female Society for Missionary Purposes with Extracts from the Report of the Society in May 1817 and 1818 and Extracts from the Reports of their Missionaries* ... (Boston: Lincoln & Edmands, c. 1818); *Massachusetts Missionary Magazine*, II, 5 (1804), 379-381; *Panoplist*, VI, 10 (1814), 334; Helen B. Montgomery, *Western Women in Eastern Lands*, pp. 11-12.

Every Christian women's organization now in the country owes a debt of grateful remembrance to the vision, initiative, and courage of this Baptist laywoman, Mary Webb; but Miss Webb herself has vanished into the obscurity which she probably would have desired, since she sought not her own fame but rather the glory of God. All that has been discovered is proof of her devotion and service in the inclusion of her name among the officers and members of many other societies, such as the Boston Fragment Society and the Corban Society. Inez H. Irwin states that she conducted "a thousand activities" from her wheelchair.[2]

The records are silent about any part played by women in the mission up to this time. But already the mission of the Protestant churches was about two hundred years old. It began simultaneously with the evangelistic activities of the chaplains of the Dutch East Indies Company in the Far East and with the efforts of the New England Puritans to convert the Indians. Ever since the work of the Mayhews on Martha's Vineyard and John Eliot near Boston, in the 1640s, missions in America seem to have been the domain of men. Only a Goodwife Daniel is mentioned as teaching school in the missions associated with Eliot. Organization in support of missions came slowly and was long confined to Great Britain. The New England Company, or Society for the Propagation of the Gospel in New England, was chartered by Parliament in 1649. The Society in Scotland for Propagating Christian Knowledge, founded in 1701, began supporting New England missions in 1732. Both societies operated through local boards of commissioners in Boston. The first local society was formed in Boston in 1747 through the influence of David Brainerd for aid to a mission to the Iroquois in New York, but soon lapsed with the termination of that mission. A renewal of that enterprise caused the creation of the Society for Propagating Christian Knowledge among the Indians in North America in 1762, but it had to dissolve because the Crown did not approve it. Samuel Hopkins and Ezra Stiles at

2 *Angels and Amazons, A Hundred Years of American Women,* p. 51.

Newport, Rhode Island, in 1773 established a missionary society intended to send Negro freedmen missionaries to Africa, but the outbreak of the Revolution put an end to it. After the Revolution, nationalism gave impetus to organization. When the Scottish Society appointed a new board of commissioners in Boston, those gentlemen refused to serve a foreign agency. They founded in 1787 the Society for the Propagation of the Gospel among Indians and Others in North America, and that same year Bishop Ettwein organized the Society for the Propagation of the Gospel among the Heathen as a general organization in support of Moravian missions.

The 1787 Society for the Propagation of the Gospel among the Indians and Others was organized according to the model of the old British societies. Its membership was limited, small in number, exclusive, and self-perpetuating. The most eminent clergymen in the Boston area were members, including all shades of Calvinist orthodoxy and the liberalism soon to be known as Unitarianism. These gentlemen were content to carry on a program the expense of which could be met by interest on their invested funds plus the collection taken at the preaching of the annual sermon. Such a society could not be the adequate instrument of the churches and the people of God in world mission. And it had long already been a true world mission which New England churchmen had in view — the evangelization of the Indians, the heathen at the ends of the earth, and now the settlers on the American frontier, so rapidly moving westward, who would be paganized unless missionaries were sent among them. The problem of the frontier exerted pressure on the one side, and on the other side the thrilling example of British enthusiasm for overseas missions stimulated American emulation. The organization of the Baptist Missionary Society by William Carey and friends in 1792, of the London Missionary Society in 1795, and of the Church Missionary Society in 1799 not only drew forth prayers and gifts but immediately stimulated new organizations. The Philadelphia Friends Aborigines Committee was founded in 1795, the union New York Missionary Society and the Northern Missionary Society in the

State of New York in 1796, the Connecticut Missionary Society in 1798, and the Massachusetts Missionary Society in 1799. Each year of the first decade of the new century would then see one or several additional societies organized. Nearly all avowed the threefold objective of frontier settlements, Indians, and overseas heathen.

However, these societies were composed of men. All that women might do was to encourage their men in such good work, to pray for the new societies, and to accompany their husbands to the preaching of the annual sermons. Women could not be content with such a limited role, even in a day when it was considered preposterous for a woman's voice to be heard in church except in the singing of psalms or hymns, when none might speak publicly on any subject in the presence of men, and when they might assemble together themselves only for a tea party and social conversation. But women had played an heroic part in the Revolution. They were interested in what was happening in the world. Their religious zeal exceeded that of men generally. Girls were beginning to be educated. Women must not be denied a part in missions and they must act on behalf of their sisters in need. Yet it took tremendous courage for Mary Webb and her companions to organize the Boston Female Society for Missionary Purposes. It required the same kind of conviction and fortitude in the same year for Mrs. Hannah Stillman, wife of a clergyman, and "a few high minded and kind hearted women" to found the Boston Female Asylum for orphan girls when "prompted to step beyond what was then considered to be the limit of female duty."[3]

Bostonian example was powerful in the land, and the women of Boston knew it. The example they set would be followed by others. The Female Society was speedily copied in a chain reaction through New England and beyond. Within the year Congregationalist women who wanted a specifically denominational auxiliary to the Massachusetts Mis-

3 *An Account of the Rise, Progress, and Present State of the Boston Female Asylum, together with the Act of Incorporation, etc.* (Boston: pr. by Russell & Cutler, 1810); [Jedediah Morse], *Reminiscences of the Boston Female Assylum* (Boston: pr. by Eastburn's Press, 1844).

sionary Society organized the Boston Female Society for Promoting the Diffusion of Christian Knowledge. By 1803 mention of the Female Association of Hampshire County, which supported the Hampshire Missionary Society, shows that organization was taking place in the Connecticut River Valley. In the principal town of northwestern Connecticut, Litchfield, the Female Society in 1804 copied the constitution of the Hampshire County society. The movement crossed the Berkshires, and the editor of the *Panoplist* marveled at the foundation of the Female Charitable Association of Whitestone, New York, in what less than twenty years earlier had been an unsettled wilderness. Now the frontier had passed on and Whitestone women were collecting funds for work among settlers far away. Other societies are mentioned in the Berkshire towns of Stockbridge, Pittsfield, Great Barrington, and Sheffield. *The New York Missionary Magazine*, the *Massachusetts Missionary Magazine*, the *Connecticut Evangelical Magazine*, and the *Panoplist* before 1812 carry news articles about, or report contributions to various societies from, other women's societies in Reading, Westfield, Newburyport, Northfield, Westbrook in Massachusetts; Norwich, Hebron, New Haven, Hartford, Willington, Woodbury, Windham, Coventry, Stamford, Saybrook, the North Consociation of Litchfield County in Connecticut; Rindge in New Hampshire; and Rutland and Ludlow in Vermont.

The parent society in Boston endeavored to give some direction to the movement. The Female Society in 1812 published in the *Massachusetts Missionary Magazine* an "address to the female friends of Zion" requesting correspondence from the other societies to be sent to Miss Mary Webb and proposing that they all meet for concerted prayer on the first Monday of each month. By 1814 cordial response had been received from forty societies in Vermont, New Hampshire, Rhode Island, Massachusetts, Connecticut, New York, Pennsylvania, and Ohio. By 1818 the number of societies in correspondence and concert had mounted to ninety-seven. Miss Webb had adapted to the women's groups the widespread practice of the friends of missions in uniting in a Concert of Prayer for Missions on a given night in each month.[4] They followed the example of the parent society in the application of their funds, mostly for literature for the frontier mission work, and nearly all of them related definitely to one or the other of the general missionary societies.

When funds increased, many of the societies made gifts for a variety of missionary purposes. Miss Webb's Boston Female Society during its first two years gave all its collection to the Massachusetts Missionary Society. Then from the third year on for at least a decade, the proceeds were equally divided between Congregationalist and Baptist causes, the Massachusetts Baptist Missionary Society having been founded in 1802. Gradually the scope of giving increased. To the provision of Bibles and literature for the frontier there was added Bible translation abroad. One year the entire offering went to the Baptist missionaries at Serampore, Bengal, India, for their tremendous program of translation and publication of the Scriptures in Oriental languages. Foreign missions in general were given support after 1810. Then in the 1816-17 season the whole of the income began to be devoted to the employment of two missionaries to "the poor and vice-ridden" of Boston. In 1829 the Society either became purely Baptist or a Baptist group separated from it, adding Baptist to the name, observing October 9, 1800, as the date of founding, and retaining the constitution slightly revised.[5]

It was the Cent Societies with their simple membership requirement of dues of fifty-two cents a year which proliferated most rapidly and widely. The *Massachusetts Missionary Magazine* for June, 1804, carried this announcement.

---

4 See note 1. On the related societies: *N. Y. Missionary Magazine*, I-IV (1800-1803); *Mass. Miss. Magazine*, I-V (1803-1808); *Panoplist (and Miss. Mag.)*, I-IV (1808-1812); *Conn. Evang. Magazine*, I-VII, n.s. I-V (1801-1812). On Concert of Prayer for Missions see R. Pierce Beaver, "The Concert of Prayer for Missions," *Ecumenical Review*, X, 4 (July 1958), 420-427.

5 *Constitution of the Boston Baptist Female Society for Missionary Purposes, organized Oct. 9, 1800, Constitution altered and amended, Dec. 1829* (Boston: True & Greene, 1830).

TO THE FRIENDS OF RELIGION

"A SINGLE cent, where Millions are necessary to carry into effect the benevolent designs of our Fathers and Brethren, who are engaged in sending the Gospel to lands unenlightened with its genial rays, may appear, at first view, small and inconsiderable: — but, should the Friends of Zion adopt the Plan of contributing only One Cent a week! and recommend the same Practice to their friends and connexions; it is presumed a very handsome sum may be annually collected, without inconvenience to individuals.

The design of this Institution, is, to procure Bibles, Dr. Watts' Psalms and Hymns, Primers, Catechisms, Divine Songs, Tokens for Children, etc.

Mrs. John Simpkins requests those who are disposed to encourage this Work, to send in their Names, with their Money, Quarterly, or as shall be most agreeable to them; — and she will engage to deposit it with the Treasurer of the Massachusetts Missionary Society, for the important purpose of aiding in that very laudable Institution."

The editor added his commendation.

This CENT INSTITUTION, "small and inconsiderable" as it may seem, promises to be very productive. Though only of about two years standing, it has already brought to the aid of the general design of the Missionary Society, nearly *eight hundred* dollars. As the knowledge of it extends, the number of subscribers to it increases. It is a female Institution, laudable in its design and simple in its principle; and as such it is ardently recommended to general patronage and attention. Our SISTERS, in town and country, will gladly embrace an opportunity to contribute, in so easy and eligible a way, to the salvation of immortal souls, and the advancement of their REDEEMER'S kingdom. One Cent a week is certainly but a trifle for almost anyone to contribute; and in almost any place, would a generous individual undertake to procure subscriptions, and to transmit the monies to Mrs. Simpkins, who has so worthily stepped forward in this business, a considerable sum might no doubt be collected. The ocean is supplied by rivers, made up of small streams. *Remember the widow's two mites.*

At first subscription papers were circulated in and around

Boston. Then the pennies flowed in from a wider area. In May and August, 1805, $472 and $501.38 were acknowledged. By the spring of 1806 about $1,800 had been received and transmitted by Mrs. Simpkins. The total for the first seven years came to more than $3,000. At the annual meeting of the Massachusetts Missionary Society in May, 1811, gifts from the Cent Society during the year were reported at more than $1,200. What the women's mites could do is shown by this accounting in the *Panoplist* of November, 1810.

The following is an abstract taken from a memorandum of books purchased for distribution, with money contributed to the Cent Society by Ladies in Boston, Charlestown, Salem, Newburyport, and many other towns in their vicinity.

In 1807, 1808, and part of 1809 were purchased and sent into different parts of the country for distribution, the following books, the prices of which are not subjoined, viz.

Bibles	155
Testaments	256
Watts' Psalms and Hymns	386
Hymn Books	13
Watts' Divine Songs	780
Catechisms	200
Spelling Books	74
Primers	226
Life of God in the Soul	100
School of Good Manners	100
Token for Children	125
Miscellaneous volumes	45
	2460

Pamphlets, more than 200

In part of 1809 and 1810, the following books have been purchased at the annexed prices.

318	Bibles, which cost	$225.25
174	Testaments	52.50
208	Watts' Psalms and Hymns	85.00
432	Primers	15.00
48	Spelling Books	7.00
217	Small religious books for children	16.33
1379		$401.08

Expenses of boxes, transportation,
loss by bad money, etc. 34.11
                                                    $435.19

It is difficult to tell from the reporting whether the local women had actually organized societies in some places, since the Massachusetts Missionary Society treats all contributions as coming from "The Cent Society." But lump sums from each place indicate the existence of actual societies. In addition to Boston there are reports from many towns and villages.* New Concord, Lee, and Stockbridge gave their pennies to Berkshire and Columbia Missionary Society. A number of clearly organized societies contributed to the Connecticut Missionary Society.** There is mention also of a Cent Society connected with the Connecticut Bible Society. Others gave to the Hampshire Missionary Society and to other state and regional agencies. Strangely the records of the New York Missionary Society report only two gifts from women's groups in its entire history — from the Union Society of New York in 1809 and the Female Cent Society of Huntington, Long Island, in 1816. Girls also made gifts in 1819: the New York Female Juvenile Humane Society and the Society of Young Ladies of Philon Academy.

With the advent of foreign missions after 1810, the Cent Societies began contributing to the American Board of Commissioners for Foreign Missions, and then to the Baptist and United Foreign Missionary Societies when they began to send missionaries. Soon they seem to have disappeared, and with the Female Charitable Societies gave place to foreign missionary societies. However, in New Hampshire, where the Cent Societies were organized as auxiliary to the New Hamp-

---

* Charlestown, Salem, Franklin, Northbridge, Medway, Wrentham, Weymouth, Byfield, Upton, Hopkinton, Abingdon, Pembroke, Newburyport, Bridgewater, Sutton, Middleboro, Carlisle, Uxbridge, Holliston, Sherborne, Milford, Randolph, Bucktown, Fitchburg, Needham, Dorchester, Braintree, Plymouth, Newton, Framingham, Eastport, Rowley, Beverly, Scituate, Bath, Marblehead.

**Hampton, Wethersfield, Warren, Sharon, Mansfield, Stepney, Sommers, Newington, Norwalk, West Guilford.

shire Missionary Society, they long continued an honorable and useful history. The state Cent Society was organized in 1804, and beginning with 1814 the Committee of the New Hampshire Missionary Society published annually a *Report on the Concerns of the New-Hampshire Cent Institution.* The *Report* for 1815 declares: ". . . in no state of our country has there probably been so much contributed by Females for the propagation of the Gospel, according to the number of inhabitants, and their means, as by the females of New-Hampshire." The Trustees were especially affected by receiving contributions from Societies of Female Children in Tamworth and Haverhill. The model constitution of a local society, offered in 1847, opens membership to any female over fourteen years of age paying annually one cent per week. The *Report* for 1829 states that five or six towns have regularly been supplied with preaching by the contributions of the 70 to 80 Cent Societies, together giving annually $1,500. In 1890 this Institution was reorganized as the New Hampshire Female Cent Institution and Home Missionary Union, combining work for the New Hampshire Missionary Society and the American Home Missionary Society and contributing also to other national programs. The *Report* for 1926 gave the number of local auxiliaries as ninety-three.

Ministers and laymen were highly approving of the Cent Society as a collecting agency, but as to local organizations either Cent or Charitable there was grave question in the minds of many. The contributions at least were highly appreciated. The *Panoplist* on the other hand consistently commended the Cent Society. For example, in the August, 1808, issue the editor wrote: "Though the sum to be paid by each individual be inconsiderable, yet the remarkable success with which the plan has been crowned demonstrates that it is not to be despised. . . . It is confidently hoped that this very eligible mode of aiding in the extension of the Redeemer's kingdom, which is within the compass of almost every person's abilities, will be more generally adopted, and continue to be a fruitful source to aid missionary societies in the great cause in which they are embarked." In Novem-

ber, 1810, that same magazine commended the members of
the Female Cent Society of Reading, Massachusetts, for devoting their collections to support the Cherokee Indian School
operated by Dr. Gideon Blackburn under the General Assembly of the Presbyterian Church. It earnestly recommended
"to the pious and benevolent Ladies of all our towns" the
formation of similar institutions. The Hampshire Missionary
Society centering in Northampton in its annual reports regularly paid a tribute of praise to the giving by the ladies;
for example, in 1805 "the trustees express their gratitude to
the charitable female association, and fiducially rely upon
the mercy of God, through our Lord Jesus Christ, that in
answer to the prayers and liberalities of the daughters of
our Zion, the long expected and blessed period will be has-
tened, when the seed of the woman shall bruise, effectually,
the serpent's head." The *Massachusetts Missionary Magazine*
in June, 1806, took great pleasure in reporting the *London
Evangelical Magazine's* commendation of the Cent Institution. The English journal commented: "Were such a method
adopted in England, among the female members of all religious congregations, and devoted by a committee of each
society to the missionary cause, or to any other institution
intended to promote the good of souls, what a vast sum
might be accumulated without inconvenience to individuals."

The women's fund-raising activities soon had the effect
of opening the membership of some of the previously exclusively male missionary societies to at least token female
representation. Three women were members of the Massachusetts Missionary Society in 1803 and another was added
the following year. On the other hand, records show that no
woman paid the initiation fee of the New York Missionary
Society until 1818, very near the close of its career.

The missionary societies, even with the assistance of the
women, never received enough funds to fulfill their three
objectives. The frontier moved rapidly westward and the
population was doubling in twenty years. The frontier settlements took almost all the resources of the societies. The
Indian missions languished because of lack of funds and

missionaries, displacement of the tribes, and the relentless pressure of white settlement. Although a few overseas ventures were contemplated, the societies were unable to initiate them. Eventually the famous student movement beginning at Williams College in 1806 and culminating at Andover Theological Seminary resulted in the formation of the American Board of Commissioners for Foreign Missions in 1810. The Triennial Convention of the Baptist Denomination for Foreign Missions was founded in 1814. Then through the action of the Presbyterian, Dutch Reformed, and Associate Reformed denominations the United Foreign Missionary Society of New York was launched in 1816 and became fully organized in 1817. But it was not until the announcement that the first party of missionaries would actually sail for India in 1812 that the money began to flow into the treasuries. Soon the foreign missionary enterprise raised the level of stewardship in the churches of the country to such an extent that more adequate resources became available for home missions and for many related activities.

The women at once responded heartily to the overseas call. The older Female Charitable Societies and the Cent Societies began contributing to foreign missions, and gradually they gave way to foreign missionary societies and to a lesser number of home missionary societies auxiliary to the major organizations. Already in 1812 Female Foreign Missionary Societies were founded in New Haven, New London, Stepney, and Wethersfield, Connecticut, and in Franklin and Tyringham, Massachusetts. Moreover, the women individually and unorganized generously gave their gifts to the traveling agents of the Foreign Mission Boards. Agent after agent reported tiny but significant gifts from hired girls in farmhouses throughout the land. The very first legacy received by the American Board came from one of these, the domestic servant Sally Thomas, who bequeathed her savings of $345.38. The first large bequest to the same Board came also from a woman, Mrs. Mary Norris, $30,000. The women began specializing, too, in their foreign missions interest. The Female Society of Boston and the Vicinity for Promoting Christianity among the Jews was instituted in 1816. It was widely believed that there must be an ingathering of the Jews to Christ before the vast multitude of Gentiles would come to him, and there were thought to be signs that this was about to happen. This Boston Society gave its funds to the London Society for Promoting Christianity among the Jews, and in 1828 began supporting its own missionary, Mr. Brewer, at Constantinople and then at Scutari. The Baptist Female Society of Boston and Vicinity for Promoting the Conversion of the Jews was formed in 1822. Princeton, New Jersey, had its Female Hindoo Society.[6]

There was soon also further specialization along functional lines in support of missions. The women in this were conforming to the pattern being set by the men. Most important were two types of auxiliaries to mission: Bible and tract societies, which provided literature for overseas work as well as at home, and education societies, which assisted poor youths in the expense of theological education for ministry at home and abroad. The numerous local and state Bible societies became affiliated with the national American Bible Society upon its organization in 1816. The Connecticut Bible Society enlisted girls' groups on the penny-a-week basis. The *Connecticut Evangelical Magazine* of September, 1809, carried this notice: "The young ladies desirous of contributing a mite towards promoting the important object for which the Connecticut Bible Society was instituted, agree each of them to pay at least one cent per week, to commence from the time annexed to their respective names. . . . Present number of subscribers is 152." The earliest major women's Bible society appears to be that of Philadelphia, and this Female Bible Society of Philadelphia was responsible for the organization in Boston. The Philadelphia ladies sent circular

---

6 *Constitution of the Female Society of Boston and the Vicinity for Promoting Christianity among the Jews, Instituted June 5, 1816* (Boston: Lincoln & Edmands, 1816); *Annual Reports*, nos. 1 (1817) to 43 have been seen; *Constitution of the Baptist Female Society of Boston and the Vicinity for Promoting the Conversion of the Jews, Organized, Oct. 24, 1822,* ... (Boston: Thos. Badger, 1822).

letters to various Bostonians with the effect that on September 5, 1814, fourteen ladies met at the home of Madam Mason and formed the Female Auxiliary Bible Society of Boston and Vicinity with the object "to distribute gratuitously the common version of the Bible." It incorporated in 1834. Its semicentennial report in 1864 relates that in 1816 it became auxiliary to the American Bible Society along with the Massachusetts Bible Society, thirty-one other state and local societies, and nine Female Bible Societies. The New York Female Auxiliary Bible Society, established in 1816, had its own auxiliary Association of Young Females.[7] An example of the other kind of literature society is the Hancock Female Tract Society, in Maine, founded as early as 1804.[8]

An interesting specimen of an education society adapted to peculiar local circumstances is the New Haven Female Education Society. It was reported in 1818 that this society that year assisted twenty-three indigent students for the ministry at Yale College with such articles as they needed, and all of them recommended by the Gentlemen's Charitable Association (i.e. The Education Society of Connecticut); and the Directors had met seven times for refitting and remaking various articles of clothing. The Yale boys evidently enjoyed personal tailoring to some degree. Boston had its Corban Society, founded in 1811, which declared that next to the Scriptures the most important means of extending the church is the Christian ministry, and which was to raise funds for the relief of worthy candidates. Dues were two dollars annually. The Society began with thirty members and at the time of incorporation in 1816 had increased to 119. By that time it had aided ninety-seven young men with clothing and money to the extent of $1,883.36.[9]

---

7 *Constitution of the Female Bible Society of Boston and Vicinity, with the Annual Report* (Boston: Munroe & Francis, 1816); *Annual Reports* have been seen from the 20th (1834) to 68th; N. Y. Female Auxiliary Bible Society, *2nd Annual Report* (N. Y.: J. Seymour, 1818).

8 *Panoplist*, III, 28 (Sept. 1807), 189-190.

9 *Third Annual Report of the Education Society of Connecticut and of*

The Corban and New Haven Female Education Societies combined a moderate degree of direct action with fund raising. We have seen that the Boston Female Society for Missionary Purposes eventually employed city missionaries, and the Boston Female Society for Promoting Christianity among the Jews came to have its own missionary overseas. Gradually societies for specific philanthropies and social action arose when the women could no longer be content only to pray and give pennies and a few dollars. They had to engage in what was directly mission work to them. Boston, that breeding ground of societies, got a gentlemen's Fuel Society in December, 1812, for "distributing coal among the meritorious poor," two months after a group of women had formed the Boston Fragment Society. The name came from our Lord's injunction after the feeding of the 5,000 to "gather up the fragments." Its constitution states: "The design of this Society shall be to assist in clothing the destitute, more especially destitute children, and to loan bedding and infants' garments to such mothers as are not able to procure things necessary for their comfort during their confinement. The Society solicits annual subscriptions and donations of money, old garments, and suitable articles." During the first three months the ladies gathered more than $1,500, visited extensively among the poor, and distributed more than 2,500 pieces of clothing to poor women and children in four hundred families.[10] There was also a Female Samaritan Society in the same city engaged in the same activity.

---

the Female Education Society of New-Haven (New Haven: T. G. Woodward, 1818); Act of Incorporation and Constitution of the Corban Society, Instituted September, 1811, incorporated Dec. 14, 1816, by Females of Boston to Aid Candidates for the Gospel Ministry (Boston: Munroe & Francis, 1817).

10 The Constitution of the Boston Fragment Society, together with a List of the Subscribers' Names (Boston: Repertory Office, 1813); The Act of Incorporation and Constitution of the Fragment Society . . . , Instituted October 1812, incorporated Dec. 1861 (Boston: Munroe & Francis, 1817); Panoplist, V, 9 (Feb. 1813), 429; Thomas Whitmore, A Discourse delivered in the Central Universalist Church, Boston, before the Female Samaritan Society, Oct. 26, 1828 (Boston: Trumpet Office, [1828]).

The line of philanthropy and social action which began with the Boston Female Asylum in 1800 may be said to climax in the Boston Female Moral Reform Society, which dared to combat prostitution and establish a refuge and rehabilitation home for ex-prostitutes. This Society outraged public opinion, and in its *Third Annual Report*, 1838, the members resolved: "In view of the unaccountable prejudice that exists against this Society and its unpopular character, we have great need of firmness, perseverance, and prudence. Then with a well tempered zeal through the blessing of God, our cause must prosper — it is the cause of God." At that meeting the name New England was substituted for Boston, and it was further resolved: "That in our opinion the women of Boston have never been behind any women in any section of our country, in devising and carrying forward schemes of benevolence, designed to benefit and elevate our race; therefore, we view it to be the imperious duty of New England women, to combine their energies, and concentrate their efforts, to elevate the standard of moral piety in Boston, till the influence of its reaction shall be felt in every town and village in our land."[11] The Society had five auxiliaries in Massachusetts and one in Marlboro, New Hampshire.

But in recounting all this activity in Boston, it must be acknowledged that women were active in philanthropy elsewhere, although the evidence is now scanty and elusive. The Female Association of Philadelphia for the Relief of Women and Children in Reduced Circumstances was organized in 1800.[12]

Both the multiplication of women's foreign missionary societies and the rise of action organizations intensified the

11 *Third Annual Report of the Boston Female Moral Reform Society, Oct. 3, 1838* (Boston: Geo. P. Oakes, 1838). The city mission work of the Boston Female Society for Missionary Purposes gave rise also to a similar Penitent Females Refuge in 1818. *Sixth Report of Directors of the Penitent Females Refuge, Dec. 1824* (Boston: [1824]). But all the directors are men!

12 *Constitution of the Female Association of Philadelphia for the Relief of Women and Children in Reduced Circumstances* (Phila.: Jane Aitken, 1803).

debate over the propriety of women's religious associations. Some minister encouraged the women in sermons and articles, although warning them to keep within certain bounds. Two sermons of 1814 are illustrative of the annual discourses preached before the women's societies. Walter Harris, pastor of the church in Dunbarton, preached to the Female Cent Society of Bedford, New Hampshire. His text was Luke 8:1-3, on certain women ministering to Christ of their substance. The preacher declared that from this text we may gather the sentiment that it is the will of our Lord to make use of the efforts of women and their friendly aid in support of his cause on earth. "Though God has made known, that it is his will that females should not be public teachers of religion, nor take an active part in the government of his church on earth; yet much may be done by them to assist and forward the preaching of the Gospel, and the propagation of religious knowledge in the world; and thus promote the Redeemer's interest." Above all they can persevere in prayer for the success of the gospel and the enlargement of the church, for blessing on the work of ministers and missionaries. They can encourage and strengthen ministers. They can instruct children and youth in religion and morality. They can discountenance vice and immorality and encourage good works and morals. They can contribute of their worldly substance for preaching, Bible distribution, and the like. Remember the widow's two mites. The Cent Institution is engaged in a good cause which will finally succeed, and all who engage will have a sure reward.[13]

Ethan Smith, minister in Hopkinton, New Hampshire, preached to the ladies of the Cent Society in his town on Proverbs 31:29: "Many daughters have done virtuously, but

13 Walter Harris, *A Discourse delivered to the Members of the Female Cent Society, in Bedford, New-Hampshire, July 18, 1814* (Concord: Geo. Hough, 1814). In this same year Archibald Alexander in *A Missionary Sermon, Preached in the First Presbyterian Church in Philadelphia on 23rd May, 1814* (Phila.: Wm. Fry, 1814) urges the General Assembly to undertake a foreign mission and affirms that the interest and liberal giving of the women will go far to support it.

thou excellest them all." After discoursing in general upon women doing virtuously and excelling, he affirms that there are peculiar objects at times which demand special attention and in which virtuous females may unite to great advantage to aid religion and humanity. He approves not only private prayer by women, but also prayer in "females' circles." Lately females have been uniting to pray for the church, ministers, the missionary cause, the salvation of the heathen and destitute, and for the gift of the Holy Spirit. Mr. Smith goes far beyond the average person in commending virtuous females who have united in charitable associations to afford aid to the indigent and relief to the distressed, such as the Corban and Fragment Societies, to care for orphans, to provide black and white children with good instruction, both literary and religious.[14]

Constant criticism made some women uncertain about the propriety of societies. The secretary of a Female Cent Society wrote to the editor of the *Panoplist* in 1816, forwarding some money, and asking advice. Some members had become uncertain as to "whether it be right for females to meet together for prayer, on account of some apostolical prohibition." The editor replied that St. Paul did forbid women to preach or teach, and that applies to certain women of this time who are setting themselves up as public teachers and leaders of exercises in church. Such is inconsistent with the original design of the Creator, but it does not apply in the case of a few females gathered in private. If women cannot pray together, then surely they cannot read, sing, or make any observations for the edification of one another. Congregationalist and Presbyterian ministers are known generally to approve the present Female Praying Societies, and so it is assumed that it is permissible for ladies to pray at missionary meetings.[15]

However, all preachers to the societies were not so approv-

---

14 Ethan Smith, A.M., *Daughters of Zion Excelling. A Sermon preached to the Ladies of the Cent Institution, in Hopkinton, New-Hampshire, Aug. 18, 1814* (Concord: Geo. Hough, 1814).

15 *Panoplist*, VIII, 12 (1816), 256-260.

ing. The Rev. Ward Cotton preached in 1816 to the Female Society in Boylston in Aid of Foreign Missions. He was evidently one of those who disapproved foreign missions and feared that money would be diverted from home missions. He gave offense by lecturing this "foreign" society on the necessity of supporting the more needy cause of domestic missions, since "For the aid of missionaries among the heathen, vast sums are pouring into their treasury from every direction." He warned his hearers who were "but little acquainted with the devices and intrigues of men" to beware of those who would lead them from the paths of duty and peace. What he was alluding to is not clear, and this preacher made it worse when the sermon was printed by adding what was supposed to be an explanation in a footnote. It only further beclouds the issue. He claimed that "a certain party" seeks to promote its designs by aid of women, and that female societies have been founded with supposedly good objects, but actually to strengthen a certain party. So, females, beware! and stay out of all kinds of politics, and "study to be quiet."[16]

The Rev. David T. Kimball was more approving and encouraging in his 1819 sermon at a joint service of two female societies in Ipswich, Massachusetts.[17] Women in every succeeding period of church history have imitated the great service which women had rendered to St. Paul and the apostles. Such women, the preacher stated, are entitled to the affectionate and respectful remembrance of Christ's friends, especially of his ministers. Women are under strong and peculiar obligations to promote Christianity. It raised them from their low and servile state to their present condition.

---

16 Ward Cotton, *Causes and Effects of Female Regard to Christ; Illustrated in a Sermon, delivered before the Female Society in Boylston, for the Aid of Foreign Missions, at their Request, October 1, 1816* (Worcester: 'Wm. Manning, 1817).

17 David T. Kimball, *The Obligation and Disposition of Females to Promote Christianity. An Address delivered June 15, 1819, before the Female Education and Charitable Societies of the First Parish in Ipswich* (Newburyport: Ephraim W. Allen, 1819).

Just contrast the situation of women in Christian lands with those in pagan and infidel regions. Women remain at the Lord's Table, when men in large numbers retire and do not partake in the sacrament. They have accomplished much by the fruits of their pens and by their prayers. Women show respect for ministers. They also instruct the rising generation in Christian doctrine and precepts. They make free-will offerings and practice benevolence with regard to the good causes of the day, such as the missionary, education, and charitable societies. In affirming these things, the preacher remarked that he intended no adverse reflection on the other sex.

Typical of the ministers in the foreign mission constituency, and showing the liberalizing influence of the overseas mission upon its supporters, is the famous Presbyterian divine and mission leader, Dr. Ashbel Green of Princeton. He still maintained many of the traditional limitations on women, but his views are far advanced beyond those which prevailed twenty years earlier. He could even contemplate women serving as missionaries although unmarried, if properly guarded and directed by men. He preached before the Princeton Female Society in 1825.[18] The text was Mark 14:8, our Lord's word about the woman who anointed him with the alabaster jar of ointment, "She hath done what she could." Dr. Green proceeded to tell the women what they could and could not properly do. Mary, the anointer, was limited and bound by her sex. There are things which women may not do — which are clearly improper for them to undertake. Females have a "shrinking delicacy" which renders them unfit for command, and which subjects them to the rougher sex. The Spirit of Christ speaking through St. Paul laid down the rule, now in force without exception, that women may not be public teachers and preachers in an assembly promiscuously composed of both sexes. Moreover, the efforts of women to

---

18 Ashbel Green, *The Christian Duty of Christian Women, A Discourse delivered in the Church of Princeton, New Jersey, August 23, 1825, before the Princeton Female Society for the Support of a Female School in India* (Princeton: Princeton Press, 1825).

promote and expand the Christian religion must be limited by the means at their command and the opportunities presented. What they give, with few exceptions, comes from the pockets of their husbands and fathers, so they must first consult those men. Because of this fact, it is a noble expression of Christian benevolence when women "cheerfully sacrifice superfluous expense in dress or equipage," or make articles for sale, or otherwise manage to save something and give it for missions.

Nevertheless, there is much that Christian women may do for the spread of their faith. Actually they may do whatever is not expressly prohibited. They can apply religion in all duties of life. They can instruct children and pray with them, particularly in the recently introduced Sunday schools. They can use their influence as mothers and sisters. (Green has nothing to say about their influence as wives!) Women may also promote the Savior's cause by measures of a private nature, especially by devising, suggesting, and recommending schemes of benevolence the execution of which naturally must be left to the men. They can personally render services to ministers and missionaries. It is their special privilege to carry instruction and piety into the families of the poor. It is permitted for women to associate together for prayer and to take part in missionary concerns, most especially fund raising. Now at this time even Female Missionary Societies have been formed; and women support Bible, Tract, Education, Jewish mission, and other specialized societies, along with orphans' and widows' homes. Dr. Green was being exceedingly liberal for his day when he said of the women, "By the intervention and aid of ministers of the Gospel, and of pious and discreet laymen, their missionaries may be selected, and missionary services be assigned and inspected, without any trespass on the rights of men, or the delicacy of women."

By the 1820s women were generally conceded the right to organize for fund raising, for prayer, and for educating themselves and their children with respect to mission.

II

WOMEN ENTER THE
FOREIGN MISSION

AMERICAN WOMEN RALLIED TO THE NEW CAUSE OF OVERSEAS
mission with enthusiasm. In it they would soon find a role
of ministry and status denied them in the churches in the
homeland. The rule of marriage was as strong among Protestant mission agencies as that of celibacy in Roman Catholic
orders, institutes, and congregations. There just could not
be a mission without women. And women were the most
numerous and faithful supporters of the cause, and their
contributions were vitally needed for the enterprise. Yet once
again women were kept subordinate to men, and the single
women had to struggle long and persistently for the opportunity to serve.

It was noted in the first chapter that news of the sailing
of the first party of missionaries to India in 1812 led immediately to the formation of at least six Female Foreign
Missionary Societies in Massachusetts and Connecticut be-

fore the end of that year. Spontaneous organization came rapidly, while many older societies also became devoted to this cause. Many societies declared themselves to be auxiliaries to the American Board, and then to the Baptist, United, Methodist, and other societies as they were founded. Societies of the American Board were most numerous and most widely diffused. By 1818 there were fifty principal auxiliaries in cities and counties with 250 allied local associations, male and female.[1] Systematic promotion of fund-raising auxiliaries began, however, only with the coming of Rufus Anderson, then just graduated from Andover Seminary, to the Board rooms in Boston in 1823. The young man published his plan of organization in the *Missionary Herald,* and then set out to achieve it.[2] Immediately connected with the Board were large Auxiliary Societies, intermediary between headquarters and local Associations in towns, parishes, and school districts. It was intended that as far as possible there should be pairs of Associations, male and female. Anderson said frankly at the time, and forty years later once again, that more money would be raised by having the Associations thus paired. Also this was "the manner least objectionable," for men and women would be kept separate, especially in solicitation of funds. The Auxiliaries were composed of representatives from the gentlemen's Associations only, and Dr. Anderson admitted that women should have been admitted to them, but again the need of separate collectors for the sexes seemed to the officers of the Board to make their representation undesirable. The women actually responded first to Anderson's promotional effort, and the first three Associations formed were the Old South, Park Street, and Union Female Associations in Boston, all organized in November, 1823. It required about four years to complete the scheme of organization, and then for more than a decade it ran on its own momentum.

---

[1] *Panoplist and Missionary Herald,* XIV, 1 (Jan. 1818), 25-28; Rufus Anderson, *Memorial Volume of the First Fifty Years of the ABCFM,* p. 183.

[2] *Missionary Herald,* XIX, 11 (Nov. 1823), 365-368; Anderson, *Memorial Volume,* pp. 183-184.

A list of Associations in 1839, after fifteen years of operation
of the system, shows the following distribution.[3]

States	Men's Associations	Ladies' Associations	Total
Maine	63	45	108
New Hampshire	92	86	178
Vermont	91	83	174
Massachusetts	222	209	431
Rhode Island	0	1	1
Connecticut	151	152	303
New York	96	26	122
New Jersey	36	17	53
Pennsylvania	69	18	87
Maryland	3	0	3
Dist. Columbia	5	0	5
Virginia	10	4	14
Ohio	81	35	116
North Carolina	0	1	1
South Carolina	3	2	5
Georgia	1	1	2
TOTAL	923	680	1,603

These Associations were affiliated with fifty Auxiliaries or
Missionary Societies of cities, counties, or districts. There was
an average of four collectors to each Auxiliary and about six
thousand local collectors appointed by the Associations themselves.

This system needed what it never got — strong directions
and cultivation from headquarters. Vitality depended upon
local dedication and leadership. It is not surprising, therefore,
to learn that the women's Associations were relatively much
more stable and active than those of the men. After twelve
to fifteen years only one-fourth of the more numerous male
Associations were actually making remittances while two-thirds
of the ladies' Associations were healthy and vigorous. Dr.
Anderson commented that the system suffered from keen
competition offered by a huge host of societies collecting for
other benevolent causes. If the Brookfield (Massachusetts)

---

[3] Anderson, *Memorial Volume*, p. 185

Auxiliary, comprising the Associations in sixteen local churches, can be taken as a typical example, for the period 1838-1841, then there were twice as many women as men supporting the enterprise.[4] In 1850 women made up 70 percent of the Auxiliary's membership. The average woman's contribution was seventy-three cents compared with the male average of $1.96 — a remarkable sum in light of the fact that scarcely any woman had an income of her own and her gift had to come out of her personal allowance or be earned by some device.

By the end of the decade of the 1850s even the women's Associations were in a sad state of decline, because of the lack of central direction in education and promotion, and, one suspects, because the women had no influence in policy which their funds implemented. The only promotional service provided by any of the boards was the publication of a magazine — the *Missionary Herald* in the case of the ABCFM — and a variety of literature, of which the annual report was most important. The chief practical resource for keeping the system going was the union, or denominational, monthly Concert of Prayer for Missions commonly observed in hundreds of towns, cities, and villages.

When the Baptist Convention for Missionary Purposes was organized in 1814 and Luther Rice, returned from India, became its organizing agent, he listed in the early annual reports every female mission society of which he could learn something, regarding it as a possible contributor. The first feminine contribution came from the Wadmalaw and Edisto Female Mite Society at Charleston, South Carolina. The New York Baptist Female Society for Promoting Foreign Missions was the first new auxiliary of either men or women specifically founded for the purpose, and a committee reported to the founding Convention that "it exhibits an example of such an admirable and praise-worthy character, as cannot fail of being imitated by the charitable Ladies of other cities." The Boston Female Society for Missionary Purposes was given status as an

---

4 *Ibid.*, pp. 179-181.

auxiliary body. Rice was especially hopeful of aid from Cent
and Mite Societies, and old and new ones did contribute. He
stated: "Indeed, the great number and rapid increase of these
laudable FEMALE INSTITUTIONS cannot fail to create
emotions the most lively and gratifying — hopes and anticipa-
tions of the most ardent and animating nature." Actually fourteen women's societies were counted as auxiliary to the board
at the end of its second year.[5]

The short-lived United Foreign Missionary Society between
1817 and its merger with the American Board in 1826 enlisted
the support of both Male and Female Auxiliaries. Its record
books show women's organizations, usually called Female
Missionary Societies, numbering thirty-two, along with forty-
one Female Cent, Mite, Charitable, and Benevolent Societies
not auxiliary also contributing.[6] The auxiliaries were found
in New York, New Jersey, Pennsylvania, and a few in North
and South Carolina. The members were women of the three
supporting denominations, Dutch Reformed, Presbyterian,
and Associate Reformed. Twelve women were life members of
this Society, both married and single. Numerous pastors were
given life memberships by the women and young ladies of
their congregations. There were fourteen such cases in 1818.
The Synod of the Reformed Church in America in 1822 requested the pastors and congregations to form auxiliaries of
the U.F.M.S. and of Synod's Committee on Domestic Missions.
There were societies in both the Reformed and Presbyterian
churches on Cedar Street in New York City. The Reformed
Church promoted Cent Societies not for foreign missions but
for support of the Theological Seminary in New Brunswick.

Methodist women's work for world mission also had a back-

---

5 *Proceedings of the Baptist Convention for Missionary Purposes, Phila-
delphia, May 1814*, pp. 28, 34; Baptist Board of Foreign Missions, *1st
Annual Report, 1815*, pp. 15-16; *2nd Annual Report, 1816*, pp. 70-93.
Other societies are mentioned in the *American Baptist [Missionary]
Magazine*, N.S. I (1817), 31-33, 69-71, 178.

6 United Foreign Missionary Society, *Treasurer's Book, Auxiliary
Societies*, and *Societies Not Auxiliary*, 3 manuscript volumes, in the
American Board Archives in Houghton Library, Harvard University.

ground of earlier Cent Societies, in this case usually called Mite Societies. They had been fostered by Bishop Asbury. The scholarly and careful historian of Methodist missions, Dr. Wade C. Barclay, says of missions in general: "Missions were one of the chief means of opening up to the women of the American Churches increased opportunity for participation in church and community life." And of the Mite Societies in particular, he states: "As some of the missionary agencies were interdenominational, the local 'mite societies' afforded women opportunity for communitywide activities." Mary W. Mason (Mrs. Thomas Mason) organized the most influential of the Methodist mite groups, the Female Mite Society of New York, and she gave inspiration and leadership in mission work to Methodist women and others.[7]

Mite society activity proved to be only preparatory to Mrs. Mason's greater achievement on behalf of foreign missions. The Missionary Society of the Methodist Church was founded in April, 1819, and approved by the Church the following year. Its first auxiliary was founded before the Society had received official recognition. Mrs. Mason on July 5, 1819, gathered together in the Wesleyan Seminary on Forsyth Street a group of women from all the Methodist churches in the city and they organized the New York Female Missionary and Bible Society. The foundress remained for many years the First Directress. There were twenty-four "managers," one from each church. The secretary informed the denominational Society of the creation of its female auxiliary in these words: "I have the pleasure to inform you, that a number of females in this city, with a desire to cultivate their feeble aid to the benevolent purposes of your institution, have formed an association. . . . Although our number was small in the beginning, we have reason to be encouraged with the present prospects of the society, and are not without hopes, that we shall

---

7 Wade C. Barclay, *History of Methodist Missions*, I/II, 41-42; anon., *Consecrated Talents, or the Life of Mrs. Mary W. Mason* (N. Y.: Carlton & Lanahan, 1870).

not be an entirely useless branch of the parent institution."[8]
The Society flourished and especially supported Mrs. Ann
Wilkins and her work in Liberia. It was the model for other
women's organizations among the Methodists. Eventually,
however, it declined because the official system of denominational control and promotion worked against it. There was a
dislike of any such intermediary organization between congregations and denominational treasuries, every church being
expected to send every cent and as large a sum as possible to
the treasurer of the Missionary Society, in this particular
instance. So at length in 1861 the New York Female Missionary
and Bible Society dissolved.

Dr. Barclay reports that references to women's missionary
auxiliaries among Methodist churches are "few and scant," but
that they do show that there were organizations similar to the
New York one in the various principal cities, such as Boston,
Philadelphia, and Baltimore.

Baltimore was the location of the most notable and successful of the Methodist women's organizations. It had a very
specific purpose made apparent in its name, The Ladies'
China Missionary Society.[9] The Methodist China mission was
launched in 1847 when the first party of missionaries was sent
to Foochow. The next March, 1848, Dr. Stephen Olin preached
a missionary sermon before the Baltimore Conference. After-
wards he suggested to Mrs. Anna L. Davidson that this would
make an excellent cause to which women could rally. Following preliminary approaches by her to the pastors and to
influential women, an organization was effected, and the first

---

8 Methodist Missionary Society, *1st Annual Report*, mss., quoted by
Wade C. Barclay, *op. cit.*, I/I, 292, see also p. 317; Mrs. C. C. North,
"Female Missionary Society of the Methodist Episcopal Church [of New
York," in *Historical Sketches of Woman's Missionary Societies in America
and England*, ed. Mrs. L. H. Daggett, pp. 95-97. The first home missionary
organization of Methodist women was also organized in New York in
1844 to support a mission to Germans in the city, the New York Ladies'
Home Missionary Society.

9 Isabel Hart, "Ladies' China Missionary Society, Baltimore," in
Historical Sketches of Woman's Missionary Societies, ed. Mrs. L. H.
Daggett, pp. 100-108.

annual meeting held in January, 1849. Once again a woman's society encountered official opposition because it deviated from the "system," even though its offerings went to the Missionary Society. Only about $300 a year could be raised until 1858 when it met a great challenge and its membership manifested new zeal. A missionary, Dr. Wentworth, presented the crying need for special work for women and girls and challenged the Baltimore ladies to provide $5,000 for the erection of a female academy. Fortunately, he got the appeal sent through the official denominational Board with a pledge that the Board would "accept their services in this respect, and execute their will." The Missionary Society even offered to advance the $5,000 if the women would pledge to pay it. The challenge was accepted, and in October three young women sailed to open the new school. New life and vigor came to the Ladies' China Missionary Society.

Missionary Wentworth wrote to the ladies: "It strikes me that the Baltimore Female China Missionary Society, has found its appropriate field of labor. You have toiled and sacrificed years for China, now Providence has furnished you with a specific object of interest inside China, inside the general mission, the church at Foochow, it is no less than the elevation of your own sex, through the medium of your own sex." This is a most discerning observation, and remarkable for a man to make at that time. Women's work for women and children was the focus of American feminine missionary interest and concern, and the cause which they would support to the utmost. Because of neglect of this concern by the general boards and societies, the women would eventually be led into revolt and separate organization.

Isabel Hart in retrospect and reflection wrote: "Thus we were led to attempt the solution of this mighty, puzzling problem of missionary labor in the East, viz: how the women could be reached and rescued and redeemed, — a problem which, soon after, others with wiser heads and stronger hands took up, — a problem in the solution of which the women of all Christian denominations are now more or less engaged, realizing that therein largely lies the solution of that other problem which the Master on Mt. Olivet put into our hands, viz: the salvation of the race."[10] After the Woman's Foreign Missionary Society of the denomination was organized for this very purpose, the Baltimore ladies voted on March 6, 1871, to merge with it and became its Baltimore Branch.

There was only one society organized as being of denomination-wide scope in the first half-century of the American overseas mission. This was the enterprise of the Freewill Baptist women. This small denomination of Free Baptists arose in the eighteenth century under the leadership of Benjamin Randall, and stood for "freedom of thought, freedom of the will, free grace, and free communion" over against New England Congregationalist and Baptist Calvinist orthodoxy. The wives of its pioneer itinerant preachers achieved a most remarkable record of heroic self-sacrifice. The Free Baptists originally, in contrast to their neighbors, granted women full liberty "to exercise their ability in public." They served as church clerks and messengers to yearly meetings. They were even given status as preachers. Mrs. Mary Savage of Woolwich, Maine, was the first of these. Then, however, after a few decades, they were affected by the prevailing cultural mores and views and the women ceased to have voice and office. Their historians give credit to the Women's Rights movement launched by Elizabeth Cady Stanton, Lucretia Mott, and Mary Ann McLintock in 1847 for reviving their initiative.

Already in 1841, inspired by a visit by Missionary Eli Noyes of India, Mrs. Ann Winsor founded the first local Free Baptist Woman's Missionary Society at Providence, Rhode Island. The New Hampshire Yearly Meeting held its sessions at Lisbon in June, 1847. The wives of the ministers and some laywomen were there with their husbands, but had no part in the meeting. Time was heavy on their hands, and they spent it in conversations. Their mutual intercourse led to a decision to attempt to assist home and foreign missions by raising funds and awakening interest. Then and there they organized the New Hampshire Yearly Meeting Benevolent Association, and

---

[10] *Ibid.*, p. 106.

adjourned to meet at the General Conference of the denomination at Sutton, Vermont, the following October. On October 13 at Sutton thirty-four women organized the Freewill Baptist Female Missionary Society and agreed to take weekly offerings. A public meeting was held with men attending, presiding, and speaking, but all men had to pay an extra fee for missions! At the meeting of 1850 it was agreed that since the Society was auxiliary they would dispense with the office of treasurer and pay all money directly to the denominational Missionary Society. They would persuade the pastors to preach on missions once in three months. In 1854 they began an effort to get all women in the churches to pledge one cent a week even where there were no auxiliaries. There was a change of name in 1863 to Freewill Baptist Ladies' Systematic Beneficence Society. Annual meetings were held until 1867. There were local auxiliaries, but only the Penobscot (Maine) Yearly Meeting Freewill Baptist Missionary Society endured to unite with the new denominational society founded in 1873. The denominational women's society gradually petered out as its leaders died. The chief reasons for its decline were the lack of all financial power and of any voice in policy in the general missionary program, and the inability of women to play a public role. The only women who ever took an active part in the public meetings over which men presided were three missionaries, Mrs. Sara P. Bacheler, Mrs. C. P. Noyes, and Miss Lavinia Crawford. Women could not work well under such restraint.[11]

The women workers for missions had one other objective besides raising funds and diffusing knowledge of overseas missionary activity. It was the enlistment and training of girls of all ages and younger boys, hoping thereby to bring up successive generations steadfastly devoted to the evangelization of the heathen. When Luther Rice visited Richmond, Virginia, in 1818, he learned that the Female Missionary Society had organized a Juvenile Female Cent Society and was also

---

[11] Mary A. Davis, *History of the Free Baptist Woman's Missionary Society,* pp. 9-22.

fostering something similar among the boys. He preached the annual sermon before the girls' society and their friends when the collection was brought in. He commented: "The fact, too, that the little girls from 6 or 7, to 12 or 14 years old, had formed a society, to save from the purchases of little delicacies their mites to assist the glorious object of giving the knowledge of the gospel to all the world, and that their lovely example was producing something similar among the little boys, could not fail to awaken emotions peculiarly delightful, anticipation the most lively and interesting." There were, for example, connected with the United Foreign Missionary Society the Young Female Mite Society of Raccoon, Pennsylvania, and the Juvenile Female Foreign Missionary Society of Fishkill, New York. There was an Association of Young Females auxiliary to the New York Female Bible Society. Similar girls' and young ladies' organizations, sponsored and fostered by their mothers and elder sisters, abounded in New England, especially in connection with the American Board. Girls were early taught the requirements of female decorum as prescribed by public opinion, and this sometimes inhibited the young women. Thus at Jericho Center, Vermont, where there was a lively Ladies' Cent Society and a Female Religious Society, the Rev. John Dennison in the spring of 1812 proposed forming a Young Ladies' Society; but there was an apparently insurmountable obstacle, their trepidation at having to offer public prayer! This was overcome when the pastor agreed to offer prayer. Gradually some of the young women learned to lead in prayer. But the girls grew older and apparently younger ones were not brought in, and eventually the two female societies united in a single Cent Society.[12]

New England had a type of institution directed toward the missionary education of children, which appears to have been peculiar to that region. This was the Maternal Association. The first of these was the work of Mrs. Edward Payson in

---

[12] *4th Annual Report of the Baptist Board of Foreign Missions, 1818*, p. 192; Records of the Ladies' Cent Society, Jericho Center, Vt., mss. in the Congregational Library, Boston.

Portland, Maine, in 1815, and the second was begun the following year in Old South Church, Boston. Not all of these were expressly concerned with missionary education, for some stopped short of the specific missionary commitment and were content with the general purpose of such a society. The Maternal Association in Dorchester (Massachusetts), founded Christmas Day, 1816, is such an example, but its constitution well states the basic character of any Maternal Association.

> We whose names are hereunto subscribed, aware of our highly responsible situation as Mothers and as professing Christians and sensible that without the divine blessing all our exertions in behalf of our children will be of no avail, have determined to form ourselves into an association for prayer in which we propose to commend our dear offspring to Him who has graciously said "suffer little children to come unto me and forbid them not for of such is the kingdom of Heaven," and to beseech Him to give us a spirit of wisdom and understanding that we may discern the proper time and manner of administering reproof, correction and instruction in righteousness — It shall likewise be our object as we have opportunity to seek out little orphan children and endeavor in a suitable manner to direct their attention to that glorious Being who styles himself the Father of the fatherless and the God of all such as put their trust in Him and we shall feel ourselves bound to attend not only to their spiritual but also to their temporal concerns and where it is not in our power to relieve them to recommend them to some Benevolent Institution whose object it is to supply the wants of the poor and destitute. We shall also endeavor to set before our children a pious example and to see to it that our walk and conversation correspond with our precepts and instructions. With a view to engage in these important duties we agree to adopt the following *rules*, taken in part from the Constitution of the Maternal Association in Portland.

The fourth rule states that once in three months the members may bring their female children between four and fourteen years of age to the meeting, at which "the exercises shall be of such a nature as may seem best calculated to interest the feeling and instruct the minds of the children." Nine girls were brought to the third monthly meeting, and what a ghastly program was inflicted upon them! They were addressed upon the importance of an early acquaintance with their God and Savior, on the peace and comfort it would afford them through life and death. They were regaled with accounts of the pious lives and striking deaths of children, and finally preached a sermon![13]

The average Maternal Association, however, was much concerned with the missionary education of girls and boys. The Constitution of the Maternal Association of Jericho Center, Vermont, directs that girls from four to fourteen and boys from four to twelve years of age be brought to special meetings in January, July, and October. It was the prevailing custom that these be missionary instruction programs. In many cases the children raised money for the education of a heathen child, although in most instances this term would cover a Christian child in a "heathen" land. It is reported that the Maternal Associations declined after 1842 and were almost extinct in 1860, when they were revived particularly for missionary purposes. In order better to achieve this end, a Mothers' Meeting, under the auspices of the Union Maternal Association of Boston, was held for eight consecutive years in connection with the annual meeting of the American Board with permission of the Board.[13]

Given the lack of cultivation from the headquarters of the boards and societies, the want of integration into mutually sustaining national and regional organizations, the denial of representation and influence in the making of missionary policy, and even the denial of women's right to lead and speak in their own meetings in some instances, it appears most remarkable that the women persisted in raising funds, praying, stimulating general interest, and educating themselves and their children. What kept the women going decade after decade, this present writer has concluded, is the role the

---

[13] Constitution and Rules of the Maternal Association in Dorchester, and Constitution of the Maternal Association, Jericho Center, Vt., both manuscripts in Congregational Library, Boston; Mrs. L. H. Daggett, ed., *op. cit.*, p. 50.

missionary wives were playing in the enterprise overseas. Missionary matrimony was part of God's very scheme for the evangelization of the world, in the opinion of the directors of the mission boards. There could be no mission without the wives. The wives were overseas exercising a role of ministry such as no laywoman or pastor's wife in America might dare to undertake. The women in the homeland identified themselves with the wives, who were vicariously serving for them.

THE MISSIONARY WIVES

The wives of the earlier missionaries to the American Indians appear to have had no active missionary function themselves. They were simply wives according to the Puritan pattern. They made homes for their husbands, and probably most of them encouraged their men in their work. Even in such a frontier mission post as Stockbridge, Abigail Sergeant refused to live down in the Indian village and insisted on a splendid house on Prospect Hill near her parents. To be sure, the wives of the Stockbridge schoolmasters in the boarding school taught the girls domestic crafts and lived in intimacy with them. Moravian wives had for almost a century gone into the forests with their husbands and shared with the Indians in the closely knit, disciplined life of the Moravian community, and many of them had gone abroad into missionary service; but, largely German speaking and directed from Herrnhut, this activity was not widely known throughout the land.

The women first began to have a missionary function of their own when the New York Missionary Society's mission to the Chickasaws in 1799 introduced the new strategy of "the mission family." The family was comprised of an ordained minister-superintendent, perhaps an ordained assistant for general evangelism, a lay catechist who would also be a craftsman, one or more schoolmasters, a farmer, blacksmith, and other craftsmen. At least the wives of the ordained men and the schoolteachers were expected to teach the girls and women the rudiments of learning and domestic crafts, such as spinning and weaving, and to help in their religious instruction. The wives and daughters of the Rev. Joseph Bullen and Deacon Ebenezer Rice were the first women to bear this duty. This plan of the mission family was some fifteen years later fully developed in the Cherokee and Choctaw missions of the American Board and the Union and Harmony Stations of the United Foreign Mission Society among the Osages.

Moreover, by the time that the American overseas mission began in 1812, British missions in India, the South Seas, and West Africa had already been in operation for twenty years, providing a model for the Americans. The American Board looked especially to the London Missionary Society for advice, and the American Baptists to the Baptist Missionary Society and to Carey, Marshman, and Ward at Serampore. Their experience had convinced most Protestants that wives were indispensable to the success of the work. It is a happy fact that the new American wives looked to the experienced British women for guidance, not as to the conduct of wives, but as to their ministry as missionaries. Three Baptist wives on board ship en route to Colombo, Ceylon, in March, 1816, wrote to Mrs. Marshman and Mrs. Ward at Serampore:

> A knowledge of the kindness and hospitality with which our dear predecessors have been received, and entertained by you, inspires us with confidence to hope for the favor of your friendship, and that you will excuse the liberty we take, and permit us, even before we arrive at the place whither we would go, to be looking to you, as our mothers in Israel and in missionary experience, and for advice and for instruction. We are young in Christian knowledge, and, to direct and aid us in our course, we greatly need the benefit of that experience which your long and successful labors among the heathen will enable you to impart. For we feel, that in a great measure, we are ignorant of their manners and customs, of course, and of those measures which may be most likely to facilitate our endeavors to do them good.
>
> If not deceived in our motives, we have been induced to leave our beloved friends and native shores, to cross the tempestuous deep, from love to Christ, and the souls which he died to purchase. — And now we are ready, waiting with

the humble hope of being employed, in his own time and way, in building up his kingdom where he is yet unknown.[14]

The American Board's position on marriage in its first years is set forth in the *Panoplist and Missionary Magazine* in 1815 (XI, 4 [April], 178-181), justifying the sending of three wives with their husbands to Ceylon. After affirming that Ceylon is safe and government officials (not being under the East India Company) friendly to missions, and noting that British missionary wives are proving very useful there in conducting schools and are being praised for imparting religious knowledge to all classes, the article gives the reasons for the Board's decision that "missionaries should, as a general rule, live in a married state, wherever they can obtain a settled and undisturbed residence." These reasons are: All the arguments in favor of the marriage of ministers in the homeland apply still more cogently to the missionary abroad. The Christian familial and social duties cannot be exemplified before the heathen "unless missionaries, who are married to well educated and pious females, who have formed all their habits and modes of thinking in a Christian country," demonstrate those concretely in family life and general deportment. Moreover, missionary societies ought to strive to raise up a Christian population in heathen lands. It is observed that children in heathen lands are like "wild asses' colts," ungoverned, ungovernable, idle, and dissolute. Missionaries, in contrast to pagan parents, govern and educate their children, make them learned, and can fit them also to be missionaries in their turn. It is here remarked that the children of Drs. Carey and Marshman at Serampore give promise of being the first Western Oriental scholars.

Moreover, the Board believes that "the decencies of civilized life, including a just appreciation of the female character, can never be introduced among the heathen, unless by the aid of females who have been educated in a Christian coun-

---

14 Letter of Rachel F. Bradwell, Sarah M. Meigs, Susan Poor, and Sarah Richards, on the *Dryad*, March 14, 1816, *American Baptist Missionary Magazine*, I, 3 (May 1817), 103-104.

try." Peoples, such as the Hindus, who may appear to have a high culture are really still uncivilized, because, as Claudius Buchanan showed in his *Researches,* "domestic virtue and domestic happiness are unknown among them." The ABCFM missionaries at Bombay have, indeed, reported such gross and universal violations of morality and decency as cannot even be hinted at in the pages of the magazine. The experiences of all modern missionaries are decisively in favor of the rule of marriage, including those among the wild Hottentots, Caffres, and Bushmen in South Africa. The Moravians have generally been married, even among the most savage peoples. "Dr. Carey, in a conversation with one of the American missionaries on that subject, would hardly admit the POSSIBILITY of a missionary being so situated, as not to make it expedient to be married. As a general rule, he urged marriage upon missionaries as AN INDISPENSABLE DUTY."

Furthermore, the more discerning men already knew that only women could approach women in most societies, and that the wives, therefore, had their peculiar responsibility. The Rev. Jonathan Allen, preaching a farewell sermon to two of the first three missionary brides, said to them about their own ministry, not that of their husbands:

> My dear children — you are now engaged in the best of causes. It is that cause for which Jesus the Son of God came into the world and suffered and died. You literally forsake father and mother, brothers and sisters, for the sake of Christ, and the promotion of his kingdom. In this employment, you, probably, have an arduous work before you — A work that will occupy all your talents and much of your time.
>
> It will be your business, my dear children, to teach these women, to whom your husbands can have but little, or no access. Go then, and do all in your power, to enlighten their minds, and bring them to the knowledge of the truth. Go, and if possible, raise their character to the dignity of rational beings, and to the rank of christians in a christian land. Teach them to realize that they are not an inferior race of creatures; but stand upon a par with men. Teach them that they have immortal souls; and are no longer to burn themselves, in the same fire, with the bodies of their departed

husbands. Go, bring them from their cloisters into the
assemblies of the saints. Teach them to accept of Christ as
their Savior, and to enjoy the privileges of the children of God.
..... May you live to see the fruit of your labors, in the
conversion of thousands of your sisters in the east, and find
that they, with their husbands and others, have turned from
their Idols, to serve the only living and true God. And may
the Lord himself be with you, and support you, and comfort
you, and be your portion forever.[15]

The original position of the American Board on marriage
was confirmed through succeeding decades and the argument
for it elaborated by Dr. Rufus Anderson. Other American
mission agencies followed Anderson's views on marriage as on
other aspects of mission practice. After half a century he
wrote: "The experience of the Board favors the marriage of
missionaries, as a general rule, and always when they are going
to a barbarous people. Wives are a protection among savages,
and men cannot long there make a tolerable home without
them. When well selected with respect to health, education,
and piety, wives endure 'hardness' quite as well as their
husbands, and sometimes with more faith and patience." It
just is not good for man to be alone. "In a word, woman was
made for man, and as a general thing man cannot long be
placed where he can do without her assistance." "Regarding
the wife as a friend, counsellor, companion, the repository of
her husband's thoughts and feelings, the partaker of his joys,
the sharer of his cares and sorrows, and one who is to lighten
his toils, and become his nurse in sickness; the missionary
needs such a helper far more than the minister [in the home-
land]." Being a "helpmeet," companion, and mother of children is the wife's first duty, because scripturally "the center
of her appropriate sphere is, indeed, within the domestic
circle"; but generally she also may be expected "to exert much

---

15 Jonathan Allen, *A Sermon, delivered at Haverhill, Feb. 5, 1812, on
the Occasion of the Young Ladies being about to embark as the wives of
the Rev. Messieurs Judson and Newell, going Missionaries to India*, in
Pioneers in Mission, ed. R. Pierce Beaver (Grand Rapids: Eerdmans,
1966).

influence in the department of education." If her health is good the wife "may exert a propitious influence over the whole extent of infant and female education, especially if she made herself familiar with the subject before leaving her native land." In general it is further the responsibility of the wives to see to it that "the female portion of the heathen world receives proper attention."[16]

Although the wife was considered indispensable, she got little official recognition. It was her husband who was appointed "missionary" and handed the instructions. She was long designated only "assistant missionary." To be sure, that was also the lot of the unordained physicians and printers. They were all without vote in the field missions. But eventually all the lay men and women proved their worth and finally got equal status and vote.

Given this official view of marriage, it is clear why young men upon appointment tried to "select well" their teammates in mission if not already romantically committed. Many did not even start looking for a wife until after appointment was assured. It frequently happened that a young man graduated from seminary, was ordained, married, given instructions in a farewell ceremony, and sailed with his bride all in the course of a week or two. Moreover, dozens of young women accepted a marriage proposal in the same spirit. This was for some years the only manner in which a young woman could fulfill her own missionary vocation. Many a marriage began on the basis of a mutual commitment to the cause, and conjugal love developed in the course of teamwork in a common ministry. A man making a study of the health and turnover of missionaries a century later remarked that in the early period missionaries were like the animals entering the Ark — they went two by two.

The cost to the wives was heavy, carrying dual responsibility for homemaking and working with women and children, in

---

[16] Rufus Anderson, *Memorial Volume*, p. 272; "Essay on the Marriage of Missionaries," in *To Advance the Gospel: Selections from the Writings of Rufus Anderson*, ed. R. Pierce Beaver, pp. 209-217.

situations where climate and public hygiene were inimical to health. An American patriarch lies buried in a cemetery at Ningpo surrounded by the graves of seven wives. Adoniram Judson, whose health was always precarious, was thrice married. In the beginning missionaries once having sailed were expected never to return to the homeland, and although furlough visits eventually were accepted as desirable, many wives never returned home. Excepting the three Mrs. Judsons, the only mention of wives in the Dwight-Tupper-Bliss *Encyclopedia of Missions* is the frequent remark that because of his wife's health some missionary did or did not do something or other. Yet often it was the wife who was the stronger and saw the husband through sickness and trials. Many a widow remained on the field to continue her ministry alone or to marry a widower, as in the case of Sarah Hall Boardman, who became the second Mrs. Judson.

Officially the wives might be regarded by executives and Board members as necessary but subordinate and secondary; yet they were heroines to the supporting church members at home. To the women of the churches and societies they were sources of inspiration and the reason for their continued prayer and fund raising. The wives vicariously represented the women at home, working out in practice their concern for the salvation of mankind and especially their heartfelt burden of responsibility for the liberation of women in Eastern lands and primitive societies. Their work was carefully followed. Individuals and societies corresponded with them and raised funds for their projects. It is remarkable that in the midst of their heavy duties the women missionaries found time to write innumerable letters. Until her death the issues of the *American Baptist Missionary Magazine* are filled with letters of Ann Judson. While at home during her one visit for health reasons she issued an "Address to Females in America Relative to Heathen Females in the East." Mrs. E. Coleman, described as "relict of a beloved Baptist missionary who went from Boston," was reported as having general superintendence of eight or ten schools for women and girls in India, and when the Rev. Eustace Carey, son of William, visited the United

States in 1825, he spent much time in speaking on behalf of female education and collecting funds for schools. Women responded heartily. Devotion to this specific mission within the general mission helped the American women and girls persist in their efforts at stimulating interest, diffusing information, making intercessory prayer, and raising funds, even when allowed no part in directing the denominational overseas concerns.[17]

Augustus R. Buckland, in his 1895 book, *Women in the Mission Field, Pioneers and Martyrs,* writes of the British women: "At home, save to the few, they were merged in the peculiarities of their husbands." This certainly was not true of the American wives. They were personalities in their own right. They were known and celebrated. They were constantly held up to God in intercessory prayer. Every member of a female missionary society felt personally involved in their fortunes. One reason for this was that two out of the first three wives who went overseas caught the public imagination and kindled the affection and esteem of both women and men. Harriet Atwood Newell was the first American to give a life in the overseas mission. Ordered out of India by the officers of the East India Company only ten days after arrival at Calcutta, the Newells went temporarily to the Isle of France, and there Harriet died at the age of nineteen on November 30, 1813. Three decades later Joseph Tracy in his history wrote of Mrs. Newell: "The tidings of her death made a deep and powerful impression. An excellent memoir ... still continues to be read with great interest. Perhaps no early missionary, even by a long life of faithful labors, has accomplished more for the heathen, than she accomplished by consecrating herself to their cause, and dying for them before the mission had found a resting place."[18] Rosanna Nott returned home in

[17] Examples of Ann Judson's letters: *American Baptist Missionary Magazine,* I (1817), 96-97, 220-223; Mrs. Judson's *Address, ibid.,* IV, 1 (Jan. 1823), 18-20; for Mrs. Coleman and Eustace Carey, V, 7 (July 1825), 223.

[18] Tracy's reference is to Leonard Woods, *A Sermon Preached at Haver-*

1815 because of her husband's poor health. Ann Hasseltine Judson became the premier heroine of the foreign mission.

Ann or Nancy Judson was from the first taken into thousands of hearts. All reacted positively toward her on direct acquaintance or only by report. She was profoundly religious and "pious" in the meaning of her day, but friendly, outgoing, and of a happy disposition. When but a teen-age girl in Bradford Academy she had been responsible for initiating a revival in both the Academy and Bradford Church. The missionary vocation came naturally to her. She made a splendid teammate for her husband Adoniram. She sustained him in his illness, moods, and difficulties. She encouraged his studies, literary work, and evangelistic efforts. She attempted to discharge her own missionary responsibility, seeking with patience and discretion to approach the wife of the viceroy and other women. As soon as she had enough understanding of the Burmese language, she prepared a child's catechism and used it in teaching. She pressed forward toward the desired goal of education for women and girls, and she rallied the women at home to support of that task. She wrote scores of letters in promotion of the mission. When her infant son died, a hundred thousand American women mourned with her. What won the undying admiration of even the men was her courageous following of Adoniram to Ava, and her devoted and ingenious ministry to him through the two years of hellish imprisonment there and at Amarapura during the war between Great Britain and Burma. Dr. Judson's two later wives, Sarah Hall Boardman and Emily Chubbuck, were highly esteemed; but Ann possessed the love and veneration of churchwomen beyond all others. More biographies and sketches have been written about her than any other woman

---

hill in *Remembrance of Mrs. Harriet Newell . . . to which are added Memoirs of her Life,* earliest ed. seen, 4th ed. enlarged (Boston: Armstrong, 1814). Another: Timothy Dwight, *Memoirs of the Life of Mrs. Harriet Newell, Wife of the Rev. Samuel Newell . . .* 3rd Boston ed. to which is annexed a *Sermon . . .* (Lexington: T. T. Skilman, 1815).

missionary, and they still continue to be published after a century and a half.[19]

The American Indian mission did not have the popularity of the overseas work. There were no broad oceans to cross, but trails across the continent were often more dangerous and rigorous to traverse. Health conditions were frequently far worse than abroad. The death toll was high. No story of a voyage half around the earth equals in drama, hardship, and heroism the record of the first six women who crossed the plains and the Rocky Mountains, those wives of the Oregon Mission. After her death Narcissa Whitman came to hold first place among her sisters in the Indian missions, but this was due as much to the development of the widespread myth about her husband Marcus' having saved Oregon for the United States, as it was to her martyrdom.[20]

---

[19] Some titles: James D. Knowles, *Memoir of Mrs. Ann H. Judson* (Boston: Lincoln & Edmands, 1829); Arabella M. (Stuart) Willson, *The Lives of Mrs. Ann H. Judson, Mrs. Sarah B. Judson, and Mrs. Emily C. Judson, Missionaries to Burmah* (N. Y.: Miller, Orton, & Milligan, 1855); Ethel B. Hubbard, *Ann of Ava* (N. Y.: Missionary Education Movement, 1913). The most recent biography of her husband: Courtney Anderson, *To the Golden Shore, the Life of Adoniram Judson* (Boston: Little, Brown, 1956).

[20] Clifford M. Drury, *"First White Women Over the Rockies"; Diaries, Letters, Biographical Sketches of the Six Women of the Oregon Mission...*, 3 vols. (Glendale, Cal.: A. H. Clark, 1963-66), I, 25-170; also by Drury, *Marcus Whitman, M.D., Pioneer and Martyr* (Caldwell, Ia.: Caxton Printers, 1937); and *Marcus and Narcissa Whitman and the Opening of Old Oregon*, 2 vols. (Glendale, Cal.: A. H. Clark, 1973).

III

THE SINGLE WOMEN PIONEERS

Despite the valiant efforts of the missionary wives to educate girls and women and to enter the zenanas for religious conversations with secluded women, the total effect of their labors never met their hopes and expectations. They had first of all to be wives and homemakers. They bore children in large numbers and had to care for and teach them. They glimpsed the promise of what might be achieved in women's work for women and children, but they longed for colleagues who would have more freedom and who could devote themselves solely to such activity. Gradually there developed among some of the men on the fields an awareness of the need of unmarried women to carry forward this special work. However, the employment of single women grievously offended public opinion about the proprieties.

There were the gravest misgivings about appointing unmarried women and a persistent reluctance to send them overseas. Strangely, it was easier for young women to get an appointment to the American Indian mission. It seems never to have occurred to the directors of the mission boards that the Indian mission might exact a far heavier toll in wrecked health and death than overseas service. Three young women, the Misses Clark, Luce, and Johnson, were in 1820 employed as schoolteachers by the Society for the Propagation of the Gospel among the Indians and Others in North America. However, they were serving in the relative security and comfort of Charlestown, Rhode Island, and Christiantown and Gayhead, Massachusetts. It was in that year that the United Foreign Mission Society sent the first mission family to Union Station among the Osages west of the Mississippi. Six single women were members of that company: Susan Lines, Eliza Clever, Clarissa Johnson, Mary Foster, Dolly E. Hart, and Phoebe Beach. Two years later three had married men of the mission, and one had lost her sanity due to illness. The Harmony Station family, formed in 1821, included five young women teachers. The American Board also sent to the Indians seven in the years 1820 to 1822.[1]

Somehow it seemed that it would be quite a different matter to send young women across the seas to "heathen lands." There was admiration expressed for the educational work of the British and Foreign School Society and of the Juvenile Female Bengal Society, but there was shaking of heads when the former in 1820 sent Miss M. A. Cook to Calcutta. One gets the impression that when appointments were finally made the boards tried to hide the presence of these women and advertised their work very little so as to shield themselves from criticisms. For example, as late as September, 1839, the *Missionary Herald* announced the departure of a man and wife for Ceylon accompanied by "three female teachers," but does not identify them. It just did not seem to the average churchman of that day either possible or proper that a woman by herself, without

---

[1] American Board of Commissioners for Foreign Missions, *Annual Reports, 1820-1830;* see each report on an Indian mission. Society for the Propagation of the Gospel among the Indians and Others in N. A., *Report of the Select Committee, 1820,* p. 30; United Foreign Missionary Society, *3rd Annual Report, 1820,* p. 21; *4th Annual Report, 1821,* pp. 19-20.

a husband to make decisions and take responsibility, could venture to be a missionary pioneer.

Typical of the male viewpoint of the time is Daniel C. Eddy's exclamation of amazement over Eleanor Macomber of the Baptist Mission to the Karens in Burma. He wrote:

> Almost all the heroines who have gone forth from the churches of America, to dot heathen soil with their lonely graves, have been attended by some stronger arm than that of weak, defenceless woman. Many of them have had husbands on whom they relied for support and protection, and to whom they could turn with the assurance of sympathy, in hours of anguish and gloom.
>
> But Miss Macomber went out attended by no such kind companion. She resolved on a missionary life, without the offer of marriage being connected with it. No husband helped her decide the momentous question, and when she resolved, it was to go *alone*. Impelled by the Christian's high and holy motives, she determined on a course which would involve her in a thousand perplexities, and load her with a thousand cares. With none to share these cares and perplexities — with no heart to keep time with the wild beatings of her own, she crossed, a friendless woman, the deep, dark ocean, and on soil never trodden by the feet of Christian men, erected the banner of the cross.[2]

Even the great theoretician and administrator of American missions, Dr. Rufus Anderson, was reluctant to open the door to unmarried women. He wrote in 1836:

> It has been urged upon missionary societies to send out unmarried females for [female education]; which of course would imply the existence of families where these could find a home. Few however appear to be aware of the difficulties of placing the single female in circumstances to live and labor happily in pagan lands. The difficulties cannot be stated here. The result to which missionary societies and missionaries generally have been conducted is, that unmarried females should rarely be sent on missions, except in connection with families to which they are related by ties of nature or of

---

[2] Daniel C. Eddy, *Ministering Women: Heroines of the Missionary Enterprise*, 3rd ed., p. 124.

intimate and endeared friendship, and where it is known that they would be received gladly as permanent members of the family. If this rule is departed from, it should only be in compliance with the wishes of some particular family or missionary station, and the person should be selected as far as may be in the manner they shall propose.[3]

It was cruel to deny single women their own homes. Moreover, the mission board secretary evidently did not understand the misconceptions which might arise in the minds of the people in Oriental societies when single women were placed with married couples. Not long ago when the present writer was stationed in central China, at a mission compound not far away a European mission society imposed that ancient rule. A rather plump single lady was lodged with a family. The wife was very thin. It was commonly believed in that area that the pastor had two wives, one of whom he loved and fed well to the detriment of the other less favored.

Even by the time of the American Board semicentennial celebration in 1860, Dr. Anderson had moved very little from his earlier position. On that occasion he stated: "The practice of sending unmarried females beyond the seas has obtained only to a limited extent. It has been so difficult to secure for them permanent and agreeable homes, and well defined and appropriate spheres of labor in no danger of failing, that the appointments are now in great measure restricted to female boarding schools at the central points of the larger missions. Every considerable mission needs one such school, and one or two competent female teachers for its instruction."[4] Thus it is evident that despite their marvelous achievement through several decades the single women were still few and still a kind of second-class missionary. They were hedged around with restrictions. Board members were overanxious about their safety. It was difficult for them

---

3 Rufus Anderson, "An Introductory Essay on the Marriage of Missionaries," a preface to *Memoir of Mrs. Mary Mercy Ellis, etc.,* in *To Advance the Gospel: Selections from the Writings of Rufus Anderson,* ed. R. Pierce Beaver, p. 213.

4 *Memorial Volume,* p. 276.

to exercise initiative. It was the same with all the American boards and societies. It is no wonder that in the very year, 1860, when Dr. Anderson penned that statement, the women revolted and formed the first women's board.

Public opinion in the early years of the nineteenth century allowed considerably more freedom to a widow than to an unmarried young woman. Such a person could be expected to have profited by the guidance of a husband for a longer or shorter period of time, and the fruit of that experience would endure. This woman might, therefore, venture to undertake some actions and enterprises beyond the proprieties imposed upon single women, even though she no longer had that "stronger arm" to support her. The first "defenseless woman" who applied to an American mission board for an overseas appointment was a widow. Charlotte H. White is the first woman sent overseas by an American agency for service without the aid of a husband, with the exception of unknown Moravian girls whom the lot designated to be sent abroad to marry men already on the field.

Adoniram Judson and Ann, his wife, and Luther Rice had sailed for India as American Board missionaries; but when they became Baptists after their arrival, they appealed to the Baptist churches in the homeland to support them. Rice returned to promote the cause personally. The General Convention of the Baptist Denomination in the United States for Foreign Missions was organized in 1814. Its managing committee was called the Baptist Board of Foreign Missions. One of its first actions was to appoint George H. Hough, with a wife and two children, to reinforce the mission just begun in Burma by the Judsons. Hough was a printer and was ordained before departure.[5]

Soon after the announcement of Hough's appointment, the Baptist Board of Foreign Missions received a letter from

---

[5] The writer finds it interesting to discover that George Hough was printing mission literature just before his appointment. See Ch. I, notes 13 and 14.

Mrs. Charlotte H. White, dated Philadelphia, June 13, 1815.[6]
This letter briefly reviewed her spiritual biography and church
membership. She expressed her long-continued interest in
the mission overseas, which she had been supporting by her
prayers. Then the letter continued:

> Hitherto I have been excluded from rendering any service to
> the mission; but I now rejoice that God has opened a way,
> and directed my mind to missionary exertions. On the com-
> ing of Mr. and Mrs. Hough to this city, and my being made
> acquainted with them and their missionary views, my ardour
> has been revived, and a desire produced to accompany them
> to India; and I now wait for the Board to approbate my
> design. My wishes are to reside in their family in the charac-
> ter of a sister to Mrs. Hough and a sister in the Lord; —
> with them to pursue such studies as are requisite to the dis-
> charge of missionary duties; — with them to suffer the hard-
> ships of such an undertaking, and with them to enjoy in
> common the favours of that God whom we would jointly
> serve: to be to them, as the Lord may enable me, a sympa-
> thetic friend in all conditions, and to solicit and look for the
> same from them; — to apply what talents I possess wholly to
> the service of the mission, either in taking the management
> of a school, or to hold private meetings, should there be
> an opportunity, with native females, to instruct them in the
> principles of the gospel, hoping, by the blessing of God, that
> some of them will be raised from their degraded and miser-
> able condition, to participate in the riches of salvation.

Mrs. White was not asking for missionary status, but she was,
indeed, asking for full responsibility and work!

Continuing her appeal, the writer of the letter informed
the Board that while she expected to encounter trials on
the mission field, she had already known them in plenty at
home. She could in all things and circumstances trust the
goodness of God. Mrs. White stated that she had come to

---

6 On Mrs. White: Baptist Board of Foreign Missions, *2nd Annual
Report, 1816,* pp. 65, 66, 112; *Proceedings of the General Convention of
the Baptist Denomination for the U. S., 1816,* p. 112; Adoniram Judson,
Letter to Lucius Bolles, Nov. 9, 1816, in Archives of the American Baptist
Foreign Mission Society, Valley Forge, Pa.

this decision through conflicting emotions, and, having waited before the throne of grace, was convinced that Divine Providence favored it. She now had quietude of mind. She ended the letter with a prayer that the Lord by the Holy Spirit might influence the decision of the Board and enlighten and strengthen her.

This letter tremendously impressed the members of the Board of Foreign Missions. A special committee was appointed to consider Mrs. White's proposal and make a recommendation. Upon further inquiry, Mrs. White informed the committee that when she had purchased her outfit she would still have about $300 remaining from her savings. It was her intention to put this sum into the mission fund. Thereupon, the committee made an affirmative report to the Board. The full Board in turn was favorably impressed and took this action: "Resolved, that the Board hear with pleasure the desire of sister White to attach herself to the family of brother Hough, to accompany them to India, and to render service to the mission: They, therefore, do most cheerfully encourage her in the design, and trust it will be of use to the general cause. The Board also engage to support her as a member of brother Hough's family."

The merchant Edward Thompson of Philadelphia gave the party passage on one of his ships, the *Benjamin Rush,* to Calcutta. The Board as an expression of gratitude made him an honorary member. The missionaries boarded the ship at New Castle, Delaware, on December 12, 1815, put to sea on the 20th, and arrived at Calcutta on April 23, 1816. Almost at once Mrs. White's plans were drastically changed. The Americans resided for some weeks with William Carey and the English Baptist missionaries at Serampore. Joshua Rowe was one of the mission staff there. Soon Mrs. White changed her status from that of "a female attached to a missionary's family" to that of missionary wife. The Board of Missions informed the next Triennial Convention in 1817 that, although Mrs. White had confidently expected to accompany the Hough family to Burma, "her expectations, by a controlling Providence, had been disappointed." She had married Joshua Rowe with the warm approval of the English brethren, and she had gone with him to open an important new station at Digha near Patna, where she was now in charge of a large school. (Later references indicate that it flourished, and she continued in service after Mr. Rowe's death.) The Board informed the Convention that it had not incurred a single cent of expense on Mrs. Rowe's behalf, and recommended that the sum she had placed in the mission fund be restored to her. Dr. Carey had written to the secretaries of the Board: "I consider her marriage as a very providential circumstance. At Digha she cannot fail of being useful." Dr. Hinton, assistant secretary of the Baptist Missionary Society in London, had made the comment: "England and America have plighted hands, at a missionary altar, by their respective representatives, Mr. Rowe and Mrs. White. Every one augurs good from their union."

Adoniram Judson, extremely conservative with respect to women while so flexible and adventurous in many other matters, breathed a sigh of relief at the news of the marriage. He wrote a letter, marked "private," to Lucius Bolles, which contains this passage:

> Bro Hough, after considerable detention in Bengal, & some disappointment in his first attempt to get a passage, has at length, arrived. Mrs. White very fortunately disposed of herself in Bengal. Fortunately, I say; for I know not how we would have disposed of her in this place. We do not apprehend that the mission of single females to such a country as Burmah, is at all advisable. Nor do we think that our patrons would have adopted the measure, had they been acquainted with the habits & ideas of this people, & the circumstances in which we are placed. Had she resided in the same house with us, it would have been impossible to have prevented the impression on the minds of the Burmans that our preaching & practice on the subject of polygamy were directly the reverse. A man, also is here considered to own his wives, his sisters (if the father be dead), & his daughter, as a part of his live stock; & as we could have laid no other claim to Mrs. White, it is not improbable, that some Burman viceroy would have conceived it improper, that such a female should long remain without a proprietor & protector. In regard to the instruction of native women & children, we apprehend, that

if every missionary is married, as he ought to be, these departments will be adequately supplied.

The first single woman, not a widow, sent overseas was Betsey Stockton. Her position is exceedingly vague and uncertain. Factors of race and class clearly affected her situation. The American Board's *Annual Report, 1824,* lists her among the mission staff at Lahinah, Sandwich Islands, as "Betsey Stockton, colored woman, *Domestic Assistant.*" She went to Hawaii in 1822, was there attached to the family of the Rev. Charles S. Stewart, and returned to the United States with that family in 1825 when Mrs. Stewart's health failed. However, during a period of two years Miss Stockton had conducted a school, which was described as "well run."

Betsey had been born a slave within the household of Robert Stockton of Princeton, New Jersey, and when Stockton's daughter, Elizabeth, married Dr. Ashbel Green, renowned Presbyterian minister and president of Princeton College, ownership of the young girl was transferred to Mrs. Green. Dr. Green was an active member of the American Board and was to be the primary factor in the founding of the Board of Foreign Missions of the Presbyterian Church in the U.S.A., Old School. The young Black woman was given the run of the Green library, and educated herself. Her spontaneous concern for world mission was probably nurtured by association with the Greens. Betsey was made free at the age of twenty, but remained in service to the Green family. After Miss Stockton returned from Hawaii she conducted a school for Indian children in Canada and later infant schools for Black children in Philadelphia and Princeton. She was a founding member of the First Presbyterian Church of Colour in Princeton in 1848. She died in 1865.[7]

When Betsey Stockton returned in 1825 there was not one unmarried woman serving or under appointment as assistant

---

[7] ABCFM, *Annual Report, 1824,* p. 104; Charles S. Stewart, *Residence in the Sandwich Islands,* 5th ed. (Boston: Weeks & Jordan, 1839), p. 34; Hawaiian Mission Children's Society, *Missionary Album,* enlarged from ed. of 1901 (Honolulu: 1937), p. 177; John A. Andrew III, "A.D. Recalls: Betsey Stockton Early Missionary To Hawaii," *A.D.,* March 1976, p. 30.

missionary, although the Church Missionary Society of London had sent forth its first appointee of this character in 1820. Seventeen or twenty had been sent to the American Indian missions by the American Board. The United Foreign Missionary Society had employed about the same number. A very few had been engaged by others. Walter Chapin in his *Missionary Gazetteer,* published that year, included an alphabetical list of all Protestant missionaries, from John Eliot and Thomas Mayhew onward, ever known to have served under any American or European society; but he does not name even a single woman, not even a wife! But now pressure from the Marathi Mission in western India was being brought upon the American Board to send out a woman educator.

This Marathi Mission had enlarged the scope and extent of its program in 1826. The missionaries at Bombay sent a communication to the Board, in which they said: "It gives us much pleasure to state, that a good degree of success has attended the efforts of the females of the mission in getting schools for native females into operation. The first was established in February, and nine have since been added to that number." This new work urgently cried for permanent and expert supervision. No missionary wife, limited by family responsibilities and confined to one station, could undertake to do this. Miss Cynthia Farrar was then appointed by the Board, and she has the unique distinction of being the first unmarried woman sent overseas as an assistant missionary by any American agency.

Cynthia Farrar was born at Marlborough, New Hampshire, April 20, 1795, the daughter of Phineas and Abigail Farrar. She made her profession of faith and joined the Congregational Church in August, 1815. After she completed studies at Union Academy at Plainfield, New Hampshire, she taught school for some time in her native state and then in Boston. Jeremiah Evarts, corresponding secretary of the Board, made a very careful search for a mature, experienced, successful teacher with Christian faith and administrative ability. He chose Miss Farrar, and she accepted the challenge. This was in May, 1827. She sailed from Boston on the ship *Emerald* on June 5 in the company of two newly appointed couples, one of the men being her cousin, the Rev. Cyrus Stone. They reached Calicut on the Malabar coast on September 21 and Bombay on December 29. She then began thirty-four years of service in the Marathi Mission. The officers of the Board had seen her sail with considerable trepidation, fearful of the public reaction. When they announced her appointment it was stated: "Such progress has been made in this important work, under the direction of English ladies in Bengal, and so prosperous a beginning has been witnessed at Bombay, as to afford great encouragement to perseverance in a branch of labor so auspiciously commenced." Miss Farrar was to fulfill the highest hopes and expectations.

Most Hindu fathers were at this time bitterly opposed to education of girls. When girls were enrolled in school little cooperation of the parents could be expected. The pupils were frequently withdrawn for holidays, or because mothers wanted them at home, or because they were to be married and sent to their mothers-in-law, there to be trained in the traditional manner. More than a decade after Miss Farrar's death it was said of her: "It was chiefly by gaining the love of her pupils, and making it pleasant for them to attend her school, that Miss Farrar could keep them long enough to learn to read, and to acquire a little knowledge of that truth which has done so much for women in Christian lands." Even high-caste girls were eventually enrolled. Prominent British residents of Bombay, including the governor, encouraged and supported this American missionary. Archdeacon, later Bishop, Carr gave Miss Farrar funds raised by an English society for the education of girls. She established and directed some schools for that society as well as for the mission. Then her health broke, and she returned to the United States in 1837 for two years of furlough.

When she had regained her health, Cynthia Farrar returned to India in 1839. She was now transferred to Ahmednagar. There she organized new schools. In 1846 there were four day schools with more than a hundred pupils. Some enlightened high-caste men in Ahmednagar were impressed with Miss Farrar's accomplishments, and in 1851 invited her to organize two schools for their daughters and other girls of the same social status. However, when these schools were making good progress, a Brahmin teacher employed in them became a Christian. The sponsors then withdrew the girls and closed the schools. Miss Farrar then continued to direct mission schools, and eventually a large primary and secondary school was erected upon the foundations which she had laid. She died at Ahmednagar on January 25, 1862, at the age of sixty-seven. Many hundreds of Hindu women paid her tribute by attendance at her funeral. She bequeathed her possessions to the Mission.[8]

A precedent had now been set by the appointment of Miss Farrar. Rumbles of disapproval not having reached earthquake proportions, the American Board the next year, 1828, dispatched to the Sandwich Islands (Hawaiian) Mission the Misses Maria C. Ogden, Delia Stone, Mary Ward, and Maria Patten. The officers explained to the Board's constituency: "The single females will have it in their power, with the ordinary blessings of heaven upon their well-meant endeavors, to comfort and aid the wives of the missionaries, in their various cares and domestic duties, and to improve the condition of the native females. This last is an object of great importance, and, if faithfully pursued, will abundantly repay all the labor bestowed upon it." A few more were sent to Hawaii in the 1830s. Those words "to comfort and aid the wives of the missionaries, in their various cares and domestic duties" reveal a constant danger to the welfare and work of the unmarried women. Lodged in the homes of married couples and expected to lend a hand there with domestic duties, a domineering or selfish or thoughtless missionary wife might make the single woman into a domestic drudge, perpetual baby-sitter, or teacher of the household children. Friction sometimes resulted, but on the whole the single women, while doing their part in the home, were too strong-minded and too committed to their own ministry to allow themselves to be used.

8 ABCFM, *Annual Report, 1827,* pp. 28-29; *Annual Report, 1828,* p. 23; Vinton Book, mss., I, 138; *Missionary Herald,* XXIII (1827), 225-226; XXXV (1839), 189-190; LVIII (1862), 133; American Marathi Mission, *Report for 1862,* pp. 3-6; *Memorial Papers of the American Marathi Mission, 1813-1881* (Bombay: Education Society's Press, Byculla, 1882), p. 62.

The Congregationalist-Reformed-Presbyterian partnership in the American Board sent only a small company of single women forth to the fields, but more than the agencies of other churches. Orpha Graves was assigned to Bombay in 1834; and Rebecca Williams and Betsey Tilden went to Beirut in the following year. Adeline White sailed to Singapore in 1834; Azuba C. Condit to Borneo in 1836; and Mary E. Pierce to Bangkok in 1839. Eliza Agnew, Sarah F. Brown, and Jane E. Lathrop were the three unidentified "female teachers" who went to Ceylon in 1839. Fidelia Fiske was the first unmarried woman to enter Persia, or Iran, in 1843. The three ABCFM women, Eliza Agnew, Fidelia Fiske, and Maria Abigail West, who went to Turkey in 1852, are the only American single women whom Messrs. Dwight, Tupper, and Bliss deemed important enough to include in their *Encyclopedia of Missions* along with the Misses M. A. Cook, Amelia Ann Wallinger, and Mary L. Whately of England, and Deaconess Charlotte Pitz of Germany. Miss Whately might be designated as of Ireland, since although born in Suffolk, England, she spent most of her pre-mission years in Ireland where her father was Archbishop. More will be related about these three Americans. Up to the semicentennial year, 1860, the American Board had appointed 691 females compared with 567 males, according to the tabulation of Dr. Rufus Anderson. The difference of 124 between the two figures represents unmarried women. However, his lists contain the names of 137 single assistant missionaries, and at least one more is designated only as a wife, which status she later assumed. Of these women 108 served in the several American Indian missions, and thirty overseas. Eleven were serving in foreign fields in 1860, and only four in the Indian mission under the Board.[9]

Some of the thirty single female assistant missionaries were Reformed and Presbyterians as well as Congregationalists. Eliza Agnew, for example, was Presbyterian, and Miss Condit Reformed. The Board of Foreign Missions of the Reformed Church in America withdrew from the ABCFM

---

[9] *Memorial Volume*, pp. 234, 236, 417-432.

and began direct sending of its missionaries in 1854; but in the interval before the formation of the Woman's Board it sent only the Misses Harriet and Louisa Scudder to the Arcot Mission in India in 1854 and 1855, and Miss Caroline E. Adriance to Amoy, China, in 1859. After the Presbyterian division in 1836 the "New School" remained in the American Board until the Presbyterian reunion of 1870.

The Baptists sent their first two single women to Burma in 1832 a few months apart, first Sarah Cummings and then Caroline Harrington. Eleanor Macomber was the third. She is in many respects the most remarkable among the pioneers, for she had the courage and determination to venture outside the limited role of teacher and educational superintendent which the men set for the women.[10] She was an evangelist and church organizer. Miss Macomber had first served her apprenticeship in missions in the Baptist work with the Ojibways at Sault Ste. Marie, Michigan, but her health failed in her fourth year there. She was appointed to the Burma Mission for work among the Karens in 1836, and arrived at Moulmein that autumn. However, she had no intention of lingering in a major station. Her persuasion of the men to permit her to go "into the jungle" must have been almost a miracle. Dong Yhan was selected for her residence, and the Rev. S. M. Osgood went there with her to obtain a site for a house and arrange for its construction. There was a festival and all the chief persons were drunk, and little could be done. Osgood departed and Miss Macomber was left alone, but she had courage and ability and succeeded beyond all expectations. The response of the Karens was remarkable. Within a few months Eleanor Macomber had gathered a church of more than twenty persons and laid the foundations for a permanent establishment there. The author of her biographical sketch commented: "Indeed, the spectacle of weak, friendless, lone woman removing from Maulmain to Dong Yhan, and there, with no husband, no

---

[10] Daniel C. Eddy, *Ministering Women: Heroines of the Missionary Enterprise*, pp. 124ff.

father, no brother, establishing public worship, opening her house for prayer and praise, and gathering schools in the midst of wild and unlettered natives, is one of full moral grandeur. The idea of performing such a work alone, the idea of a defenceless woman going into a besotted nation, among a drunken, sensual people, and lifting them up to the privileges of a refined faith, a pure religion, is an idea worthy of an angel."

Miss Macomber visited the tribes throughout an extensive surrounding area, accompanied by a few converts. Her first convert, a man, was baptized only a few weeks after her arrival. Other men soon made profession accompanied by their wives. Dr. Adoniram Judson baptized three daughters of the chief. Remembering his expressed views about single women, one wonders at his possible thoughts. Nuclei of other congregations were formed in other places. Enemies, especially Burmese Buddhists, tried to burn Miss Macomber's house while she was in it. The Karen chief protected and aided her. The lone missionary left her remote post to visit colleagues at Moulmein in March, 1840, and then went on a two weeks' trip to a community of Pwo Karens. She returned to Moulmein on April 4 happy and in good spirits, but the next day suffered a virulent attack of "jungle fever." She died on April 16, 1840, aged thirty-nine years.

The other functioning Baptist sending agency, the Freewill Baptist Missionary Society, dispatched its first single woman worker, Miss Sarah P. Merrill, of Stratham, New Hampshire, to the Bengal-Orissa field in 1846. Within the year she married the veteran O. R. Bacheler. Next year Miss Lavinia P. Crawford of Awkright, New York, went to the same field.

The Protestant Episcopal Church carried on a mission of fraternal aid to the church and people of Greece, especially dedicated to the advancement of education. Mrs. Hill, wife of the missionary, appealed to the Domestic and Foreign Missionary Society for help in her schools in Athens. Miss Mary Briscoe Baldwin volunteered for the post, and went in 1832. A grandniece of President James Madison, she was born in the Shenandoah Valley of Virginia on May 20, 1811. She had just passed through a period of serious reflection after becoming disillusioned with the social life of the Virginia aristocracy. The young woman of twenty-one reported: "For some years I had felt a great desire to be directly engaged in some Christian work, especially in extending the knowledge of the Gospel among my fellow creatures, such as is the privilege of clergymen to do, but, being a woman, I could not possibly enter the ministry. Next to this my thoughts turned to the life of a missionary, and this seemed a position far too high and heavenly for me to attain and enjoy." The call from Athens then coincided with Mary Baldwin's missionary vocation. In view of the poverty of her pupils, Miss Baldwin put much emphasis on the sewing department of the school. When the court of the new independent Greek monarchy was set up in Athens, the skill of her pupils was in tremendous demand, much to their economic benefit. She trained young women of the upper classes as teachers in hope of further stimulating schools for girls. When she returned to Athens from her furlough visit home, Miss Baldwin established a boarding school for the daughters of the elite and spent most of her private income on its support. It fulfilled her strategic aim: that school became tremendously influential in the development of the education of girls in Greece.

Miss Baldwin demonstrated her versatility and initiative when Athens was crowded with Cretan refugees in consequence of the revolt against Turkey in 1866. She operated an extensive refugee program, comprising day and Sunday schools, feeding the starving, teaching women and girls to sew and knit, providing them with material, and marketing their finished products. With the termination of the refugee program, she then after a third of a century in Greece removed to Palestine, where her nephew was American consul at Jaffa. There a Scottish woman, Miss Arnot, was conducting a school for girls. Miss Baldwin assisted in that school until her sight failed. After successful medical treatment, she taught in a school for boys established by her nephew.

Money was needed to erect an adequate building, and she returned to America for the first time in twenty-five years to raise the money. She succeeded in that effort, but during one of her speaking engagements suffered a serious fall which left her in pain through her remaining days. Despite this infirmity, Mary Briscoe Baldwin continued teaching until her death on June 21, 1857, after forty-two years of creative service.[11]

Miss Baldwin was one of the most effective pioneers, and she is typical of them. She showed imagination, initiative, and versatility. She could meet an emergency, such as the Cretan refugee problem, with a program of action as well as any man might have done. A good teacher and educational administrator, she could move outside that field to which men wanted to limit the women, into other areas of service. Like some few others among the single women missionaries, she was so devoted to the cause that she invested her own private income in the work. Here is also that common determination to work until the very end. Few of the single women returned home; most of them died on the field of their labor.

The Methodist Missionary Society commissioned the first single woman about the same time as the Baptists and Episcopalians. The Methodist mission to Liberia had grown out of the work of the American Colonization Society which endeavored to repatriate freed slaves in Africa. West Africa at this time was still drinking up missionary lives as a sponge absorbs water. The first missionary, Melville Beveredge Cox, died of "African fever" immediately upon arrival in 1833. Within two months two couples and Miss Sophronia Farrington were appointed, and arrived at Monrovia on New Year's Day, 1834. Miss Farrington was a teacher employed by the Boston auxiliary to the general Methodist Missionary Society. One of the couples died within three months. The health of the other couple broke, and they returned home.

---

11 Annie Ryder (Mrs. J. T.) Gracey, *Eminent Missionary Women*, pp. 71-77.

They tried to take Miss Farrington with them, telling her that the Board would not keep her there. She, too, had been laid low with the fever, but, sick as she was, she could not see the mission abandoned. She wrote home: "But I have absolutely refused to go. Though to be cut off by the board would be somewhat trying, as it would seem like being turned away from my father's house; yet should they do it, I resolve to trust. ... I laid my life on the altar in leaving America, and I am willing that it should remain there." Remain she did, but by the time reinforcements came in October, including Eunice Sharp, a Negro teacher, Miss Farrington had undergone more than twenty attacks of African fever. She was in such a state of danger that there was no alternative but to return home in April, 1835.[12]

Despite the health peril there was no lack of volunteers. The following year, 1836, Dr. S. M. E. Goheen, the first of the Methodist medical missionaries, gave an address at the Sing Sing, New York, Camp Meeting. Dr. Nathan Bangs, secretary of the mission board, was also present. After the physician had made his address, Dr. Bangs was handed a note. It read: "A sister who has little money at command gives that cheerfully, and is willing to give her life as a female teacher if she is wanted." She was wanted most urgently! Without delay Mrs. Ann Wilkins was commissioned and sailed for Liberia, June 15, 1837. This young widow of thirty was born in New York state in 1806 into a family of Methodist and Friends background. It is said that she was a "born teacher." She began teaching in the Liberia Conference Seminary at White Plains, but after two or three years fulfilled her ambition to establish a boarding school for girls. She started the school at Millsburg with a few orphans and with a learning-and-labor curriculum. This became eventually Millsburg Female Academy, the very first American Methodist school for girls overseas. Poor health sent Mrs. Wilkins home twice for recuperation, in 1841 and 1853, but each time

---

[12] Wade C. Barclay, *History of Methodist Missions*, I/I, 329-336; J. M. Reid, *Missions and Missionary Society of the Methodist Episcopal Church*, I, 67; *Christian Advocate and Journal*, VIII, 36 (May 2, 1834), 142.

she returned as speedily as possible. She came back to the
United States again in a terminal illness and died November
13, 1857, at the age of fifty-one.[13] She left a permanent contribution with the people, the Methodist Church, and especially
the women of Liberia.

The Methodist Missionary Society also in 1837 and 1840
sent Miss Marcella Russell and a Mrs. Jenkins to Rio de
Janeiro and Buenos Aires respectively. The latter is described as "a strong character." She refused to submit to
the authority of the superintendent in certain matters, and
her connection with the society was terminated.

Pioneering is a relative matter, chronologically and in
types of work. Edwina and Lottie Moon are true pioneers,
although they did not enter service until after the period
under consideration. Public sentiment about the proprieties
for single women remained unchanged far longer in the
South than other sections of the country. The Moon sisters
courageously blazed new trails for Southern women when
they went abroad in 1872 and 1873. Some areas opened late
to missionary penetration. China, for example, was closed
to foreign residence and missionary work until the European
powers forced the cession of Hong Kong and the opening
of five ports in 1842. Meanwhile missions were directed to
the Chinese in the vast area collectively known as the South
Seas, and British single women were the first in the field.[14]
Miss Mary Newell was the first. She went to Malacca under
the London Missionary Society in 1827, and later married
the celebrated German missionary Karl Gützlaff. She was
succeeded by a Miss Wallace whose expenses were met by

---

13 Barclay, *History of Methodist Missions*, I/I, 338-339; Annie R. Gracey,
op. cit., pp. 45-49; Abel Stevens, *The Women of Methodism*, pp. 275ff.

14 *Female Agency among the Heathen, as recorded in the history and
correspondence of the Society for Promoting Female Education in the
East* (with an address by W. B. Noel) (London: Edward Suter, 1850),
pp. iii-v, 10, 32, 219, 242, 265, 269, 272; D. MacGillivray, *A Century of
Protestant Missions in China (1807-1907)* (Shanghai: Amer. Presbyterian
Miss. Press, 1907), p. 257, but there are inaccuracies here. Miss Grant did
not go to Singapore until 1843, and Miss Gillett, not Miss Fay, was the
first single woman sent by an American agency (p. 301).

some Scottish lady friends, and she in turn became Gützlaff's wife. The Society for Promoting Female Education in the East sent one of the original members of its governing committee, Mary Aldersey, to open a school for Chinese girls in Sourabaya, Indonesia, in 1837. She transferred to Singapore and thence to Hong Kong, finally to Ningpo, and must be credited with the establishment of the first school for girls in China proper.

The Episcopalian Eliza Jane Gillett was the first American unmarried woman sent to China in 1845, just three years after the ports were opened. However, she never reached her assigned station, but married Dr. Elijah Coleman Bridgeman and transferred to the American Board. Her arrival in the unmarried state seems to have been forgotten, and one usually finds Miss Lydia Mary Fay, also an Episcopalian, designated as the first American single woman missionary in China.[15] She carried on a full program in Shanghai after her arrival in 1850, beginning with a number of day schools and a boarding school for boys, a teacher training class, and the personal care and teaching of a few girls — all who could be gathered. Her boarding school developed into St. John's College. Miss Fay was the first woman missionary to gain recognition as a sinologist, and she collaborated with Dr. S. Wells Williams in his *Syllabic Dictionary*. She died October 5, 1878, at Chefoo while on a visit there intended to improve her health.

There is complete mystery as to how to account for the relative fame of the several pioneer missionaries — and for the obscurity in which some are lost. The latter is generally to be accounted for by the reluctance of the mission boards to employ such women and to advertise their work. The present writer would venture the opinion that Eliza Agnew and Fidelia Fiske became the most famous of the educators largely because Miss Agnew lived so long that the cumulative effect of her ministry became widely known, and because the intimate relationship of Miss Fiske to Mt. Holyoke Seminary (College) focused attention on her. Certainly their achieve-

---

15 Gracey, *op. cit.,* pp. 66-70.

ment was high and they are typical of the educational pioneers.

When Miss Eliza Agnew (born at New York City, February 2, 1807), a Presbyterian under the American Board, went to the boarding school for girls at Uduville (Oodooville), Ceylon, in 1839 it was already well established and had ninety-five pupils. She served as principal until retirement in 1879, but remained in residence until death on June 14, 1883.[16] She died at the age of eighty-four without once returning home on furlough. The continuity of her effective administration along with her ability as an inspiring teacher gave the school a high reputation and great influence. What above all made her a power throughout the Jaffna peninsula was her annual itineration to all church centers and her visitation of her former students in their homes. She was a spiritual mother to a host of women and girls, and the cumulative effect of her influence was unequaled in the pioneer period. In contrast to the schools for boys in Ceylon and India at that time, which had few converts, more than six hundred of Miss Agnew's pupils became Christians. Her obituary states: "She was well called 'the mother of a thousand daughters.' All her pupils loved her as a mother, and nearly all of them claim her as their mother in Christ, and she was permitted to see their children to the third generation walking in the ways of the Lord." "She probably led more brides to the marriage-altar than any other person living."

Miss Fidelia Fiske was born into the highly religious home of Rufus and Hannah Fiske on a farm at Shelburne, Massachusetts, on May 1, 1816.[17] Her uncle, Pliny Fisk (Fidelia restored the e), was an early missionary to Palestine, and she showed great interest in missions from early childhood. Fi-

---

16 *Missionary Herald*, LXXIX, 9 (Sept. 1883), 330; Gracey, *op. cit.*, pp. 179-185.

17 D. T. Fiske, *Faith Working by Love: as Exemplified in the Life of Fidelia Fiske* (Boston: Congregational Publishing Soc., 1868) (see pp. 415-416 for Rufus Anderson's testimonial); *Missionary Herald*, LX, 9 (Sept. 1864), 257-260.

delia went through a conversion experience in 1830 and was admitted to membership in the local Congregational church. Her education in local schools terminated in more advanced education at Mary Lyon's Mt. Holyoke Female Seminary, where she graduated in 1842. Miss Lyon immediately brought her back as a teacher. But it was that very autumn when the founder fostered a serious concern for the foreign mission among her students. This appeared to be a providential preparation for the visit of Dr. Justin Perkins in January, 1843, seeking two recruits from the school for the seminary for girls at Urumiah recently left in bad shape by the death of Mrs. Grant. That evening at prayers Miss Lyon asked all volunteers to write a note and deposit it at a certain place. Within an hour forty notes had been placed there! The briefest note was that of Miss Fiske: "If counted worthy, I should be willing to go." It was hard for the principal to give up her promising teacher, but she recommended her above all others. However, the widow mother, Fidelia's sister, her pastor, other relatives, and friends all opposed her. In view of this array of sentiment, she withdrew her offer. Another was appointed in her stead, but at the last was unable to go. Miss Lyon went to Shelburne with her young friend and won the mother's consent. Time was short. The Mt. Holyoke girls sat up all night sewing for her. She sailed with Dr. and Mrs. Perkins, Miss C. E. Myers, and others on March 1, and arrived at Urumiah on June 14.

The day school, under Miss Fiske's direction, now became a boarding seminary, and soon began to exert a powerful influence among the Nestorian women. The first indications of the great revival in the Nestorian Church in 1846 began in that school. Other revivals occurred in 1849 and 1856. Like other teachers met in this chapter, Miss Fiske visited homes, gathered women together in her home, and held meetings in villages. The graduates of the seminary established three annual district women's assemblies, where they came together for a day of worship, prayer, and discussion of practical concerns and evangelism. Miss Fiske founded the Maternal Association with weekly meetings in

Urumiah in 1856 and gave it much attention, although she was in poor health.

Precarious health, suspected of being cancer and evidently actually a cancer of the lymph glands, finally made it appear Miss Fiske's duty to leave the school and Persia for a season. Therefore she returned home in the summer of 1857. The trustees and faculty of Mt. Holyoke Seminary asked her to be a kind of chaplain to the school and a little later offered her the presidency, which she declined. She was busy writing her "Recollections of Mary Lyon" and promoting missions as well as ministering in the seminary. However, the development of the disease which brought her home ended both hope of a return to Urumiah and her present activity. She died at her brother's home in Shelburne on July 26, 1864.

Dr. Rufus Anderson, who was — as we have seen — no enthusiast about the employment of single women, wrote one of the most generous, gracious, and discerning testimonials after Miss Fiske's death. He said in part: "In the structure and working of her whole nature, she seemed to me the nearest approach I ever saw, in man or woman, to my ideal of our blessed Saviour, as he appeared in his walks on earth." "Her usefulness was as extraordinary as her character." "I should certainly find it hard to name one, among the thousand and more who have gone forth into the missions of the Board during my official life, who has a brighter record of missionary service."

The boards and societies were reluctant to employ single women, to give them freedom of residence, and to allow them to venture outside restricted educational activities for girls and women. However, once having commissioned them, the boards did not seek to bind these women by either a permanent or term requirement of celibacy, as the Society for Promoting Female Education in the East was already doing and as the women's boards would do later. Many of these "assistant missionaries" became the second or third wife of a veteran missionary and continued to serve in their fields. Six of the women listed in Dr. Anderson's tables are shown to have married missionaries under the American Board, but some of those whose name bears the symbol *r* for "resigned," actually resigned to marry men in other missions and some even outside the missions. There is only one instance on record of a general church board and its field administrators endeavoring to put pressure on a woman to remain single. That is the case of Eliza Jane Gillett, who sailed single, became a wife, and ended her career of service as a widow.

Eliza Jane Gillett was born at Derby, Connecticut, May 6, 1805, the youngest of the nine children of a prosperous merchant. After her father's death, the young girl lived with her mother in New Haven, where she completed her schooling and where she was confirmed in Trinity Episcopal Church. She taught for two years in the school where she had studied, and then removed with her mother to New York. At the age of twenty-two Miss Gillett became principal of a boarding school for girls, and held that position for seventeen years. She was a member of St. George's Church and taught a Bible class there. Originally a sense of missionary vocation came to her through reading Buchanan's *Christian Researches in India,* and this was strengthened by further reading and the influence of her pastor, Dr. James Milnor. When the China Mission of the Episcopal Church was fully organized and Bishop W. J. Boone consecrated bishop for the missionary district, he recruited a staff of new missionaries, including three single women teachers, of whom Miss Gillett was one. She was appointed November 14, 1843, sailed December 10, 1844, and reached Hong Kong April 24, 1845. Canton was the next place to be visited. The Bishop lodged one couple and Miss Gillett in the home of Dr. Elijah Coleman Bridgman, the very first American missionary to go to China. That gentleman had just given up his intention to remain celibate and was relying upon providence to present him with a bride. The arrival of Eliza Jane seemed providential, indeed. He proposed, she accepted, and they were married in the colonial chapel by the official chaplain on June 28.

When Miss Gillett had been appointed, it was intimated by the committee of the Domestic and Foreign Missionary

Society that she was expected to remain unmarried in the
post to which she was to be commissioned. Although at that
time she had no thought of marriage, she had reacted with
spirit against what she regarded as a violation of both personal liberty and Christian liberty. When she married Dr.
Bridgman, Bishop Boone, upset by the loss of his promising
recruit, lost his head sufficiently to charge Mrs. Bridgman
"with breach of contract with the great Head of the Church."
Her reply was respectful but firm. She reminded him that
she had explicitly refused to promise to maintain celibacy
and had not bound herself by a monastic vow. It was by
the Bishop's own arrangement that she had become acquainted
with Dr. Bridgman, and she believed that the cause of mission was being advanced by her marriage with him. This
was no violation of a covenant with God. No earthly power
can be authorized to curtail Christian liberty in this respect.
So Eliza Jane Gillett became wife of the senior and most
highly respected American missionary of the day and transferred her relation to the American Board of Commissioners
for Foreign Missions. The Bishop soon got over his annoy-
ance with the woman who had married his old friend and
the two families were intimate friends until the end of their
days.

Mrs. Bridgman first taught two young girls who lived in
her home. When Dr. Bridgman had to take up residence in
Shanghai from 1847 onward on account of union Bible translation work, his wife took the two girls to the new location
to form the nucleus of a school. Additional girls were recruited by visits to homes. The school opened at Wongka
Moda in 1845. Mrs. Bridgman conducted it for fifteen years.
There are references to this as the first Protestant school for
girls in China, but Miss Aldersey's school in Ningpo seems
to antedate it by one to two years. Boarding was introduced
in 1850. Domestic crafts supplemented academic studies. The
fifty pupils that could at most be accommodated were soon
enrolled. Many girls became Christians and a number of
them married Christian youths. Mrs. Bridgman eventually

turned this institution over to the Presbyterian Mission when she left Shanghai in 1862.

Dr. Bridgman died in 1861 at a time when his wife's health was low. The next year she was persuaded to go to the United States for recuperation. While on this furlough she wrote *The Life and Labors of Elijah Coleman Bridgman,* just as in the furlough year 1852/53 she had written her book, *Daughters of China.* As she was about to return to China against the advice of friends, an accident almost took her life. She eventually recovered, sailed in 1863, and barely escaped capture by the Confederate raider *Alabama.* Peking was now open to foreign residents, and the American Board's North China Mission moved there from Shanghai. After having earlier learned Cantonese and then the Wu dialect of Shanghai, Mrs. Bridgman now learned Kuo-yü, or Mandarin. In the imperial capital opposition to the education of girls in the Western manner was even more intense than in Shanghai and South China. Nevertheless, Mrs. Bridgman once again gathered pupils, opened a school, and through those pupils made contacts with their mothers. She spent her own private income on the purchase of land, erection of buildings, and maintenance. Moreover, she gave about $12,500 toward the buildings of the Peking Station of the American Board. She received no salary during her last eight years of service.

Mrs. Bridgman's intense work wore out her frail body, and in October, 1868, she journeyed to Shanghai for rest and medical treatment. Her health improved somewhat, and she threw her energies into the development of a newly opened school for girls. Once again her own funds were heavily invested. But this final effort completely exhausted her reserve strength. She died November 10, 1871, aged sixty-six, and was buried beside her husband. She is typical of the unnumbered widows who gave their last years in faithful ministry, burning themselves out for the sake of the gospel and of women and girls who might be brought to Jesus Christ.[18]

18 *Missionary Herald,* LXVIII, 4 (1872), 109-112; *Chinese Recorder,* IV, 10 (1871), 26-263; no. 11, 298-302; Eliza Jane Gillett Bridgman, *Daughters of China* (N. Y.: Robert Carter, 1853), autobiographical.

No single or married Black women stand out between Betsey Stockton in the 1820s and Eunice Sharp in the 1830s, and the founding of the Congo Mission of the Presbyterian Church in the United States (Southern Presbyterian Church) in 1890 by the Black missionary William H. Sheppard. His wife, Lucy Gannt Sheppard (1867-1955), had a ministry of high achievement in educating girls. Four notable single women served in that mission.

Maria Fearing, born a slave at Gainsville, Alabama, in 1838, during childhood developed a desire to go to Africa. She did not begin formal education until she was thirty-three years old, and she completed the ninth grade at Talladega College, where she became assistant matron. When Sheppard was on furlough he called for recruits for the Congo mission, and Miss Fearing volunteered. She was then fifty-six years of age, and the Executive Committee for Foreign Missions rejected her as too old. However, she sold her house, withdrew her savings, and with an added $100 given by the women of Talladega Congregational Church again applied to the Committee, stating that she would pay her own expenses. The Committee appointed her, and she accompanied the Sheppards to the Congo in May, 1894. Maria so soon proved her worth that after two years the Executive Committee appointed her a regular missionary with full support. She quickly learned the Buluba-Lulua language, taught at Luebo, and then established there the Pantops Home for orphaned and kidnapped girls, where the girls lived in small cottages. She was the director until 1915. Miss Fearing died at Gainsville in 1937.[19]

Three other women who went out single married missionaries and gave excellent service. Lillian M. Thomas, a graduate of Talladega College, an able and experienced teacher, also responded to Sheppard's call and was a member of the

---

[19] Althea B. Edmiston, "Maria Fearing, a Mother to African Girls," in Timmons, Sarah L., *Glorious Living, Informal Sketches of Seven Missionaries of the Presbyterian Church in the United States* (Atlanta: Committee on Women's Work, Presbyterian Church, U. S., 1937).

same party that sailed in 1894. She married missionary L. A. De Yampart in 1908, and was invalided home in 1914. Annie Katherine Taylor, a graduate of Scotia College, went to the Congo in 1906, served first at the Pañtops Home, and then became superintendent of the Marie Carey Home at Ibanche. She married Rev. A. A. Rochester in 1911 and died at Mutoto in 1914. The most notable was the third of the trio, Althea Maria Brown.

Miss Brown, daughter of Robert and Molly Suggs Brown, was born December 17, 1874, at Russellville, Alabama, and received her early education from her father. She entered the seventh grade at Fiske University in 1892 and graduated with highest honors in 1901. She was the only woman speaker at the commencement exercises, where her topic was "What Missions Have Done For The World." Long concerned about Africa and especially the Congo, she applied for appointment to the Executive Committee for Foreign Missions after a year at the Chicago Training School for City and Foreign Missions, was accepted, and sailed on August 20, 1902. She was stationed at Ibanche. There she reduced the Bukutu language to writing and prepared a dictionary and grammar, while directing day schools, Sunday schools, women's work, children's work, and being supervisor of the Maria Carey Home for Girls. Miss Brown married Alonzo Edmiston in 1905. The couple had two sons. Illness disrupted their ministry from time to time. Returning from furlough in 1922 they were stationed at Mutoto. The mission had no funds for publication of the dictionary and grammar when they were completed, but with permission of the Executive Committee Mrs. Edmiston raised $2,000 in the United States for the purpose. She also produced hymn books, school books, and folk literature. Finally she and her husband translated and printed the entire Bible in the local vernacular. She died of malaria and sleeping sickness at Mutoto on June 9, 1937.[20]

---

[20] Julia L. Kellersberger, *A Life for the Congo; the Story of Althea Brown Edmiston* (New York: Revell, [1947]).

IV

THE WOMEN'S BOARDS OF
FOREIGN MISSIONS

WHEN RUFUS ANDERSON RETIRED AS FOREIGN SECRETARY OF THE
American Board in 1866 he said to his successor, N. G.
Clark: "I cannot recommend bringing the women into this
work; but you are a young man, go and do it if you can."
Dr. Clark did encourage the women. But by this time the
women of the churches would no longer patiently await the
enlightenment of the men who controlled the general church
boards. They were ready to act independently if necessary.
When the semicentennial of the American overseas mission
was celebrated in 1860 there were engaged in the enterprise
only five major boards and five minor ones. During the next
forty years, up to 1900, the Canadian boards were organized
and those in the United States increased to ninety-four sending and forty-three supporting agencies. Participation in foreign missions became an identifying mark of mainstream
American Protestantism. However, the great new development

of that period was the emergence of the women's boards. By 1900 there were forty-one of them in the United States and seven in Canada.[1]

The consequences of this women's movement were dramatic. Adequate provision was at last made for work with women and children. The general boards had second thoughts about that subject as well as about the employment of single women. Tremendous new financial resources were brought to the overseas work. The unmarried women missionaries became just about as numerous as the wives, and the missionary staff was predominantly female. Hundreds of thousands of American women were enlisted in a cause they passionately, intelligently, and prayerfully supported.

Many factors contributed to the new initiative in mission taken by the women. Secondary and higher education for women was certainly a major cause. Coeducation, begun at Oberlin College in 1833, and the women's colleges pioneered by Mary Lyon at Mt. Holyoke Seminary turned out graduates with broad interests and leadership ability as well as devotion to the Christian mission. All the women leaders accorded Mary Lyon a special place in the rise of the movement.[2] Gradually a new profession for women came to be recognized and given prestige, teaching. Education strengthened the women's rights movement, and participation in that cause in turn trained many women for participation in various public concerns.

Many Northern women had been actively involved in the abolition movement. Then the women of both North and South were given a passionate cause for devotion in the Civil War. The War was the most effective school for women in initiative and public affairs in the course of the nineteenth century. Women in South and North managed families and farms while their men were in military service. They or-

---

1 James S. Dennis, *Centennial Survey of Foreign Missions*, pp. 9-13.
2 An example: Helen B. Montgomery, *Western Women in Eastern Lands*, p. 8.

ganized to provide services to soldiers. The women of the North were the great force behind the Christian Commission. Some women followed their men to the front. Others nursed the wounded and disabled. Helen B. Montgomery wrote:

> In its educative force on the women of the nation the Civil War overtops all other agencies. During the awful struggle the women both North and South received a baptism of power. They were driven to organize, forced to cooperate by their passion of pity and patriotism, and in the management of the great commission for raising and distributing aid to the soldiers they discovered powers of which they themselves and the nation had been quite unconscious It is no accident that it was the decade following the close of the Civil War that saw the launching of scores of organizations, among them the Missionary Societies.[3]

British example also gave the American women a model for action. The story of separate organization for women's work begins with British response to an appeal made by an American male missionary to China, the Rev. David Abeel. This minister of the Reformed Church in America went to the China coast as chaplain of the Seaman's Friend Society in 1829, and from 1830 until his death in 1845 was a missionary of the American Board. When death was thought imminent in 1833, he was invalided home and spent some months of 1833 and 1834 in London while en route. There he persuaded some women friends of missions and the Rev. B. W. Noel of the necessity of taking direct action to organize a "female agency" since the existing societies were so reluctant to move. These acquaintances published and distributed Abeel's "Appeal to Christian Ladies in Behalf of Christian Education in China and Adjacent Countries."[4] This mani-

---

[3] *Ibid.*, p. 10.

[4] *Female Agency among the Heathen, as recorded in the History and Correspondence of the Society for Promoting Female Education in the East* (London: Edward Suter, 1850) (Abeel's Appeal, pp. 261-265); Daggett, ed., *Historical Sketches of Woman's Missionary Societies*, pp. 182-193; G. R. Williamson, *Memoir of Rev. David Abeel, D. D.* (N. Y.: Robert Carter, 1848); see pp. 135-145 for London episode.

festo on the liberty and welfare of Oriental women described
their plight and pleaded for the concern of Christians, assert-
ing that Christian education is the only practical and effica-
cious means that can be employed by ladies. Abeel listed
the stations at that time immediately open to such work
in Malaya, Java, and Siam. "China itself will, in all proba-
bility, soon be prepared for as many teachers as *all the ladies
in Christendom can send or support.*" There was then founded
in London The Society for Promoting Female Education in
the East, intended primarily "to prepare and send out pious
and intelligent women as trainers and superintendents of
native female teachers." Soon its missionaries were at work in
all those places mentioned by Dr. Abeel. Following in the
example of this society came the Church of Scotland's Ladies'
Association for Foreign Missions, 1837, and the Indian Female
Normal School Society, later called the Zenana Bible and
Medical Mission, 1852.

Fired with new zeal by the response of the British ladies,
Mr. Abeel arrived in New York bent upon effecting another
similar organization. He found a ready and able co-worker
in one of the most remarkable laywomen in the whole history of American Protestantism. She was Sarah R. (Mrs.
Thomas C.) Doremus of the South Reformed Church in
the city, an active worker and leader in every aspect of
women's concerns. Already in 1828, during the Greek war
for independence, she had organized a society for the relief
of Greek women, and she was now organizer and president of
a society in support of Mme Feller's Baptist mission at Grande
Ligne in Canada. She held several meetings of interested
and committed women, principally Reformed, and the group
prepared to organize. However, at the final meeting a letter
from Dr. Rufus Anderson of the American Board was read,
asking the women to defer organization indefinitely. Some
were for moving ahead, but out of respect for Dr. Anderson
and the American Board, the majority abandoned the project.
David Abeel, present on that occasion, exclaimed with tears

in his eyes: "What is to become of the souls of those who are ignorant of the offers of mercy and of the Bible?!"[5]

Mrs. Doremus was busy with a multitude of causes in following years. Besides working for the American Board missions and then those of the Reformed Church separately, she threw her energies into a multitude of local projects. She inaugurated a Sunday service in the city prison of New York and stimulated the organization of the Women's Prison Association. She was one of the managers of the City and Tract Mission and of the New York Bible Society. She was a founder of the House and School of Industry, of the Nursery and Child's Hospital, and of Woman's Hospital. She was one of the organizers of the Presbyterian Home for Aged Women. During the Civil War she was active in services to soldiers.

The next impetus toward organization of a women's mission society came from a Baptist source. Mrs. Francis Mason came home on furlough from the Burma Mission, where she was very successful in education of girls and women. She was an exceedingly strong-minded woman, often with weird views, extremely independent in action, and later she caused the Baptist Mission much trouble until finally her husband repudiated her views and actions. Now she sought to induce a large-scale appointment of single women to the Burma Mission. She was rebuffed by the officers of the Baptist Board, but succeeded in realerting to the cause groups of women in Boston, New York, and other centers. Mrs. Doremus took up the challenge and led the movement. The women rallied to her. The nondenominational (or interdenominational, as the women would prefer) Woman's Union Missionary Society of America was organized and incorporated in February, 1861. Mrs. Doremus remained president until her death in 1877.

---

[5] Mary E. A. (Mrs. W. I.) Chamberlain, *Fifty Years in Foreign Fields — China, Japan, India, Arabia. A History of Five Decades of the Woman's Board of Foreign Missions of the Reformed Church in America*, pp. 3-7. For a sketch of Mrs. Doremus, see Annie Ryder Gracey, *Eminent Missionary Women*, pp. 10-22.

Soon there were auxiliaries or branches in New York, Boston, Philadelphia, Chicago, St. Louis, and elsewhere.

Mrs. Mason's station of Toungoo was selected as the first location for a mission, out of regard for that lady. Miss Sarah Hall Marston went there that very same year as the first appointee of the Society. The following year zenana work was begun at Calcutta by Miss H. G. Brittan. The disruptions of the Civil War and the limitations due to solely volunteer, unpaid leadership and administration made difficulties for the infant Society. Yet within a decade its missionaries and associated national workers were engaged in Burma, India, China, Syria, Greece, and Japan. The organization of numerous denominational women's boards prevented the support expected for this Society. Nevertheless, it is the mother and inspiration of all those denominational societies and can claim a share in their achievements. This organization reported at the end of its first twenty years that it had sustained 101 missionaries in twelve stations, of whom forty-three had been sent from the United States and fifty-eight employed on the field. It had also supported 174 Bible readers and 278 children. Individual missionaries and projects in other countries had also been aided by its funds. Total income had been $741,939. A far distance from the income of a Cent Society in 1802 or 1822! There were thirty-eight active missionaries in 1965, and the income that year was $157,130.[6] After more than a century and decade of service this Society changed its name to United Fellowship for Christian Service and then in 1976 merged with the Bible and Medical Mission Fellowship. Men as well as women are employed.

The Congregationalist women of New England were the first to organize a denominational society, and they provided incentive to others. Boston again led the way. Although appreciative of the work of the Woman's Union Missionary Society, these women deemed it wiser to try to supplement the work of general church boards than to act entirely in-

6 Twenty-fifth (Silver) Anniversary of the Woman's Union Missionary Society of America for Heathen Lands (N. Y.: W.U.M.S., 1886); magazine, Missionary Link, 1861–; Daggett, op. cit., pp. 194-203.

dependently. Now the American Board was ready to meet their wishes. Dr. N. G. Clark saw the inevitable coming and wished to incorporate it into the American Board's program. He addressed a letter in April, 1867, to the leading women, proposing a form of cooperation. Under the direction of Mrs. Albert Bowker a group of women in and around Boston spent the remainder of that year in meetings for prayer and discussion and in interviewing mission board secretaries, eminent ministers, and missionaries. By the New Year they were ready to act.

Forty women of the Boston region met in the chapel of Old South Church in the first week of January, 1868, reviewed the efforts of the past months, heard a powerful address by Mrs. Clementina Butler, who with her husband was the founder of the Methodist Mission in India, and reconsidered Dr. Clark's letter. Being all Congregationalists the women adopted a resolution to form a society "cooperating with the American Board in its several departments of labor for the benefit of our sex in heathen lands"; but when they met again the next week and formally organized the New England Women's Foreign Missionary Society, an interdenominational objective was accepted. Women of the several denominations might be members and their donations would be paid to the mission boards of their respective churches. However, only Congregationalist women responded, and the next September the constitution was altered, limiting relationship to the American Board. The name was changed to Woman's Board of Missions, and the geographical limitation was eliminated.[7]

The Woman's Board of Missions was incorporated in March, 1869. The magazine *Light and Life for Heathen Women* began publication. Three lines of work were planned: the raising of funds for the support of single women missionaries

---

[7] Daggett, *op. cit.*, pp. 49-65; Kate G. Lamson, "History of the Woman's Board of Missions," typescript prepared in 1927/28, in Library of the United Church Board for World Ministries, Boston; see also American Board histories: Strong, *The Story of the American Board* (Boston: Pilgrim Press, 1910), and Goodsell, *You Shall Be My Witnesses* (Boston: ABCFM, 1959).

and for all expenses of work for women and children; the dissemination of missionary information and the fostering of the missionary spirit through local branches in churches and auxiliaries in the Associations of Congregational Churches; and the training of children for participation in the mission. The first local branch was immediately organized at Middlebury, Vermont. Missionaries were sent forth in the first year: Mrs. Mary K. Edwards to the Zulu Mission in South Africa and Miss Mary Andrews to China. Miss Myrna Proctor was the first agent of the Board stationed at the Bible House in Boston, and from 1870 to her death in 1902 Miss Abbie B. Child was corresponding secretary, developing the fifteen Auxiliaries and many local branches and generally administering the program.

There was a consensus that the country was too vast for a single society to function well nationally. Few women could afford to pay for a long trip to attend plenary or committee meetings. It was believed that regional boards might well involve many more women intimately in the work and stimulate local interest. Dr. N. G. Clark took the initiative in effecting organization of the Congregational women of the central part of the country. He visited Chicago in 1868 and called to a meeting in Second Presbyterian Church on October 27 the wives of all Congregational and New School Presbyterian pastors in the city and one hundred more from the region. The Woman's Board of Missions of the Interior was founded on that occasion. Miss Mary Porter in Peking, already in service, was adopted as the first missionary, and before the end of the year support of five others was also undertaken. The Presbyterian reunion took place in 1870, and denominational pressure was brought upon the Presbyterian women to resign and form a purely Presbyterian organization. Reluctantly they did so.[8]

A third board of Congregational women soon came into

---

[8] Grace T. Davis, *Neighbors in Christ. Fifty-eight Years of World Service by the Woman's Board of Missions of the Interior;* Daggett, *op. cit.,* pp. 66-71.

being on the West Coast, Boston being much too far away.
Local societies originally related to the Boston Board in Oakland, San Francisco, and Santa Barbara provided the nucleus.
When the General Association of Congregational Churches
met at Santa Cruz in 1873, ladies from those three branches
along with others from eight additional churches met in an
adjunct assembly and founded the Woman's Board of Missions of the Pacific. It was to cover the states and territories
of California, Oregon, Washington, and Nevada. During
the next few years this Board was practically auxiliary to
the Chicago organization, but soon it assumed a direct relationship to the American Board like that of the other two.
Later the Congregational Women of Hawaii organized the
Woman's Board of Missions for the Pacific.[9]

Dr. N. G. Clark played an influential part in the formation of the two Congregational societies, but in other cases
there was no similar initiative by the men secretaries of general boards. The women acted on their own volition. They
organized three types of societies. Some, such as the Congregationalist Boards, were independently incorporated but
were designed to cooperate in supplemental fashion with a
denominational board. Others, like the Methodist Episcopal
women's agency, were independent and considered themselves on a level of parity with the corresponding denominational general agency. Some, of which the Episcopal Woman's
Auxiliary is a prime example, were departments of the denomination completely subsidiary to the central organization.
Certain societies, such as the Methodist, were national, while
others were regional.

Two missionary wives of the India Mission were responsible for organizing the Methodist women. As Mrs. Edwin
W. Parker was leaving for furlough, a number of feminine
colleagues begged her to tell American women about the
state of Indian women and to remind them that women can
be reached only by women. Funds were urgently needed

9 *Fifty-five Years, Woman's Board of Missions for the Pacific and
Program of Jubilee Meetings;* Daggett, *op. cit.,* pp. 72-74.

to train and support helpers and to publish literature. They declared that no money could be secured from the Missionary Society of the church. Mrs. Clementina Butler was already in Boston and speaking about these matters. Just as soon as she was settled near Boston, Lois Parker began promoting the cause. Notices were sent the Methodist churches in the area inviting interested women to meet at the Tremont Street Church on March 22, 1869. A late snowstorm of blizzard proportions came down upon Boston that day, but Mrs. Parker, Mrs. Butler, and seven other ladies made their way through the drifts. They wrote a constitution, elected officers, and formally constituted the Woman's Foreign Missionary Society of the Methodist Episcopal Church. Forty-four women in seventeen states were made vice-presidents in order to involve as many persons as possible. Branches and auxiliaries were organized immediately, and, because of the desirability of decentralization, the branches came to be treated as quasi-autonomous societies federated nationally. *The Heathen Woman's Friend* began publication in May. At the first public meeting on May 26, 1869, Miss Isabella Thoburn was commissioned to service in India.

The women intended to set up an independent, equal partner cooperating with the Methodist Missionary Society. It was with considerable trepidation that the secretaries and some other men of the Society met with the women in Bromfield Church, Boston, on May 7 after the organizing to discuss relationships. The conclusion reached was that the Woman's Society, "though not auxiliary to the general Missionary Society, should work in harmony with it, seeking its counsel and approval in all its work." Fields of work, methods, missionaries, and expenditures must receive the approval of the "parent society." The General Conference of 1872 gave general approval to this arrangement and recommended that any real estate acquired abroad by the W.F.M.S. be held for it by the Methodist Episcopal Church. For more than a decade there was friction over the raising and use of funds and other matters, until the General Conference of 1884 recognized the Woman's Foreign Missionary Society as an official organization of the denomination.[10] The Society strictly limited its program to overseas regions, and refused affiliation to California women who wished to work on behalf of Chinese girls and women who were then being imported as slaves, concubines, and prostitutes. The Woman's Missionary Society of the Pacific Coast was founded in August, 1870, and entered into cooperation with the Methodist Missionary Society. Despite the uncertainties felt in some male quarters, there were officials who approved. Bishop Matthew Simpson declared: "A house is sad without either half, and it is perfect only when both are present; and this Missionary Society is but another illustration that it is not good for man to be alone."

Baptist women organized regionally. Stimulus came from the participation of many Baptist women in the Woman's Union Missionary Society, from the example of Congregationalist, Methodist, and Canadian Baptist women, from signs of greater cordiality in the denominational board, and from pressure from the fields. The officers of the American Baptist Missionary Union, having polled the missionaries and being faced with a dearth of male candidates and an abundance of applications from able and devoted women, admitted in 1869 that the Union had been in error in its policy toward single women. It announced that it would accept more but keep them limited to educational work for fear that more public employment would arouse the antagonism of Oriental men. The Baptist Convention of Nova Scotia, New Brunswick, and Prince Edward Island in 1868 commissioned their first missionary — a woman — and sent out Miss Minnie B. De Wolfe to Burma through the American Baptist Missionary Union. In 1870 Miss Hannah M. Norris was accepted, but could not be sent until funds were in hand. Miss Norris herself promoted the cause with determination and zeal. In two-and-a-half summer months she organized

---

[10] Frances J. Baker, *The Story of the Woman's Foreign Missionary Society of the Methodist Episcopal Church, 1869-1895*, pp. 13-64; Barclay, *History of Methodist Missions*, II/III, 139-149; Daggett, *op. cit.*, pp. 109-135; for W.M.S. of the Pacific Coast, Daggett, pp. 136-141.

thirty-three Woman's Missionary Circles. A Central Board of these societies was created in 1871.[11] This example was not without effect on women south of the border.

Then once again the igniting spark came from the mission field. Mrs. C. H. Carpenter at Bassein, Burma, wrote to her sister, Mrs. Alvah Hovey, wife of the president of Newton Theological Institution, proposing that she undertake the organization of women's societies auxiliary to the Union for the purpose of enlisting and supporting women teachers. Mrs. Hovey and friends sought the approval of the officers of the Union. It was granted, provided that the Union direct the work, appoint and assign the missionaries, fix salaries, and control appropriations. The women accepted such limitations. About two hundred ladies met at the Clarendon Street Baptist Church in Boston on April 3, 1871, and organized the Woman's Baptist Foreign Mission Society "for the Christianization of women in foreign lands" working through the A.B.M.U.[12]

It had been expected that women all across the country would join this Society, but regionalism prevailed. The Woman's Baptist Missionary Society of the West was formed at Chicago on May 9, 1871, and in October, 1874, at San Francisco there was organized the W.B.F.M. of the Pacific Coast. The San Francisco agency became auxiliary to the Chicago Society in 1893, but meanwhile the Oregon women had separated and formed their own Society. There was interaction and cooperation between the societies, but integration of efforts was effected by the Union, which assigned to the several organizations specific fields, stations, and institutions.

Presbyterian organization began with a home mission objective. Women members of all the Presbyterian churches

---

11 Baptist Convention of Nova Scotia, New Brunswick, and Prince Edward Island, *Minutes of the 23rd Session, 1868*, pp. 20-21, 28-29; *25th Session, 1870*, p. 34; *26th Session, 1871*, pp. 10, 12, 19, 20; *27th Session, 1872*, pp. 16-17.

12 Robert G. Torbet, *Venture of Faith*, pp. 192ff.; Daggett, *op. cit.*, pp. 13-44.

in New York City united in the spring of 1868 in the New Mexico, Arizona, and Colorado Missionary Association. Its objectives were Indian and Mexican missions and general church extension. The Presbyterian Reunion of 1870 led to a change of name and scope. Foreign missions were added and the name altered to the Ladies' Board of Missions of the Presbyterian Church. Two other societies were also organized in 1870, the Woman's Foreign Missionary Society with headquarters at Philadelphia and the Woman's Presbyterian Board of Missions for the Northwest at Chicago. Their objects were overseas and American Indian missions.[13]

Local congregational missionary societies had been of long standing in the Reformed Church in America, and had supported in turn the New York and United Foreign Missionary Societies, the American Board, the Board of Foreign Missions of the denomination, and the Woman's Union Foreign Missionary Society. Large-scale participation in the last of these seems to have delayed the formation of the Woman's Board of Foreign Missions of the Reformed Church in America, organized in 1875 "to aid the Board of Foreign Missions in the Reformed Church in America by promoting its work among the women and children in heathen lands."[14]

The organization of the Reformed Church Board completed the formation of what the women themselves called the five large boards or major boards. This number was made possible by counting all regional boards of a denomination as a single entity. Organization of the other denominational societies now came speedily. The Woman's Auxiliary of the Domestic and Foreign Missionary Society of the Protestant Episcopal Church was formed in the winter of 1871/72 following action by the Society and the General Convention

---

[13] Arthur J. Brown, *One Hundred Years, A History of the Foreign Missionary Work of the Presbyterian Church in the U. S. A.*, Bk. I, ch. III, pp. 113ff.; Daggett, *op. cit.*, pp. 157-176.

[14] Mary E. A. (Mrs. W. I.) Chamberlain, *Fifty Years in Foreign Fields*, pp. 10ff.; Daggett, *op. cit.*, pp. 75ff.; Edward T. Corwin, *A Digest of Constitutional and Synodical Legislation of the Reformed Church in America* (N. Y.: Bd. of Publication, R. C. A., 1906), pp. 830-831.

the previous autumn. Following an appeal from the India Mission, the Free Baptist Woman's Missionary Society was revived in 1873. The next year the Christian Woman's Board of Missions was established with headquarters in Indianapolis. This is the only women's board that sent men as well as women, and it was a sending society in its own right. The Woman's Missionary Association of the United Brethren in Christ came into being in 1875, the Woman's Foreign Missionary Society of the Methodist Protestant Church in 1879, and the Woman's Board of Foreign Missions of the Cumberland Presbyterian Church in 1880. Soon thereafter many others were organized: Advent Christian, Christian, Church of God, Evangelical, Reformed Episcopal, Friends, Lutheran, Reformed Church in the U.S., United Presbyterian of North America, Free Methodist, African Methodist Episcopal, Wesleyan Methodist, two more regional Presbyterian in U. S. A. societies, and the Foreign Department of the National Board of the Young Women's Christian Association. Canadian churchwomen established four Baptist, one Anglican, one Methodist, one Presbyterian, and two Congregationalist societies, all of which kept in close consultation with the sister societies and boards in the United States.[15]

Perhaps the most amazing and interesting phase of the movement was in the South, where opposition to association and action by women was far more persistent and adamant than in the North. There had been at best seventy local Baptist missionary societies in the region before the secession of 1842, but none appear to have survived. Now the women of two out of the three great regional churches organized. The ladies of the Methodist Episcopal Church, South, were first to act. A Trinity Home Mission Society in Trinity Church, Baltimore, was organized and in 1872 added foreign missions to its concern. A stalwart worker, Mrs. M. L. Kelley, called "the mother of Foreign Missions" in her denomination, next organized a society at Nashville, Tennessee, in 1873. Out of such pioneer beginnings there emerged

---

15 See the Index for a list of the societies.

in May, 1878, the Woman's Missionary Society of the Methodist Episcopal Church, South. The General Conference required that "the operations of this Society should be conducted in cooperation with the Board of Missions and subject to its advice and approval." Southern women were remarkably responsive to this lead, and in less than five years there had been established thirty-one Conference Societies with 1,112 local auxiliaries. The first missionaries, the Rankin sisters, Lochie and Dora, were sent to China within a few months after organization.[16]

Southern Baptist organization is intimately associated with Miss Lottie Moon, who well illustrates both missionary influence on the people back home and the manner in which the women moved out of stationary schools into rugged field evangelism. Charlotte Diggs Moon and her sisters Orianna and Edmonia were a remarkable trio. The elder Orianna was the only woman commissioned a surgeon (captain) in the Confederate Army. The younger Edmonia was one of the first two single women appointed by the Foreign Mission Board of the Southern Baptist Convention in 1872. Lottie had graduated in the first class of the pioneer college for women in the South, Hollins Institute, in 1857. She then had a notable career as a teacher, and had founded a new school for girls at Cartersville, Georgia, in 1870. She had felt a call to overseas service, but unmarried women were not then being accepted. The commissioning of Edmonia renewed her resolution. Gaining reluctant release from her patrons supporting the school, she volunteered for China, and joined sister Edmonia at Tengchow, Shantung, in 1873. The younger sister, however, was almost immediately invalided home. Lottie conducted a school at Tengchow, hampered by the prevailing hostility to the education of girls, but yearned to carry the gospel to the women and girls of the interior villages and towns. With tremendous strength of purpose she began such work and after 1885 devoted herself entirely to that ministry. Singlehanded she founded the church in Pingtu and itin-

---

16 Daggett, *op. cit.*, pp. 142-149.

erated widely. Knowing the need of new missionaries for effective orientation and language instruction, she made her home in Tengchow, called "Little Cross Roads," a training center for women missionaries. Miss Moon carried on a vast correspondence with women all over the South and contributed articles to denominational magazines. The secretary of the Mission Board told her: "You have the power of making people see what you think." Southern Baptist men as well as women were soon feeling the power of her pen and spirit.

Lottie Moon in the truest sense gave her life for the Chinese people. During the revolution of 1911 famine wreaked havoc throughout the Baptist mission field in Shantung, and hit Pingtu with devastating severity in 1912. The missionaries appealed to Richmond for relief funds, but the Board was burdened with debt and did not respond. Miss Moon gave most of her salary and actually starved in identification with the people. Her health broke, and she was sent home to recuperate. However, she died on board ship in the harbor at Kobe, Japan, on Christmas eve, 1912. Yet Lottie Moon lives as the "patron saint" of Southern Baptist Missions.[17]

The first local society formed in that new era was the Baptist Female Missionary Prayer Meeting in 1867 in Baltimore for the support of Bible women in the Canton mission. This led to the Woman's Mission to Women of the Baptist churches of Maryland in 1871. Then a great impetus to interest and action was given by the appointment of the first single women missionaries, Edmonia Moon and Lula Whilden in 1872 and Lottie Moon in 1873. A missionary society was formed in Richmond in aid of Edmonia Moon, while women in churches of South Carolina and Alabama gathered funds for a residence for Miss Whilden. When Lottie was appointed, a society formed in Carters-

---

17 *Foreign Missions Journal*, LXIII, 8 (Feb. 1913); Una Roberts Lawrence, *Lottie Moon* (Nashville: Sunday School Board, So. Bapt. Conv., 1927); Irwin T. Hyatt, Jr, *Our Ordered Lives Confess: Three Nineteenth Century American Missionaries in East Shantung* (Cambridge: Harvard University Press, 1976).

ville, Georgia, joined the Richmond society in providing a residence for the sisters. The cause of the women got assistance with the assumption of the executive post in the Foreign Mission Board by Dr. H. A. Tupper in 1872, and he encouraged the creation of Central Committees in the states. Masculine ideas about the proprieties for women, shared even by many women, delayed a denomination-wide organization. Then a letter from Lottie Moon published in the *Foreign Missions Journal* in December, 1887, declared that the organization of the women for missions was the imperative demand of the day.

Miss Moon proposed a week of prayer culminating in a special Christmas offering as the means of giving unity, strength, and purpose to an organization that would be auxiliary to the mission boards of the Convention. The stimulus thus given gained power from a series of editorial articles in the *Religious Herald* signed "Ruth Alleyn," actually by Miss Alice Armstrong. The Woman's Missionary Union was organized in 1888. A further appeal by Miss Moon for women workers for Pingtu provided the purpose of the first Christmas offering. It amounted to $3,315, enough to send three new missionaries. The Christmas offering was ever after called by her name, and Miss Moon stimulated it by letters and articles while she lived. Eventually it became the chief resource for the financing of the Southern Baptist overseas mission. The goal of $14,500,000 set for the Lottie Moon Christmas Offering in 1966 was oversubscribed. The 1978 offering was $35,919,605. Through the influence of the first executive secretary, Miss Annie Armstrong (1888-1906), the Woman's Missionary Union became auxiliary to both Home and Foreign Boards.[18]

Social conservatism, backed up by some degree of theological argument, restrained the women of the Presbyterian Church in the United States beyond the bounds of reason. There was persistent opposition to any organization beyond the local church. A committee report to General Assembly

---

[18] Fannie E. S. Heck, *In Royal Service;* Alma Hunt, *History of the Woman's Missionary Union.*

in 1889 revealed that thirty-nine out of sixty-eight presbyteries were on record against any such organization. This
was provoked by the fact that three years earlier Mrs. Jennie
Hanna and Mrs. Josiah Sibley had begun working for Presbyterial Societies and two were organized in 1888. The first
Synodical Society was organized in 1904. Then in 1912 the
women arranged for some favorable presbyteries to overture
the General Assembly for formation of a denominational
organization. To the amazement of the women the overture
was approved. The executive secretaries of the four Executive Committees of the church then met with representatives
of the women, planned the form of organization, and established the Woman's Auxiliary.[19]

It was not only in the South that the churchwomen were
delayed in organization, hampered in action, and restricted
in developing programs because of the long-lingering opposition of men to the public appearance and action of
women, and especially of their assumption of ministry and
administration in the churches. The church has always been
the bastion of male arrogance and power, and the men
were most reluctant to share control and ministry with the
women. A few examples will suffice. When ladies in the
Evangelical Association in 1878 provoked discussion of the
possibility of a women's society, an influential officer of the
church told them: "It will be useless to appeal to the Board,
they will not grant permission for such an organization."
Whereupon he was given the reply: "Well, they cannot prevent our gathering funds and praying for such an organization!" The request when put to the Mission Board did
meet refusal, and elicited the assertion that there was no
need of a women's organization. However, in 1880 a petition for permission to form local auxiliaries was granted,
and twenty-five were formed. The members of these societies
held a Woman's Missionary Convention in 1883, drafted a
letter to the General Conference, pleading for a place in

---

[19] Hollie P. Winsborough, *The Woman's Auxiliary, Presbyterian
Church, U. S.*, pp. 7-22.

the church for women, and asking for permission to organize a Woman's Home and Foreign Missionary Society. The General Conference gave approval, and referred the effecting of organization not to the women themselves, but to the Mission Board. That agency procrastinated for a year, and then in 1884 organized the Woman's Missionary Society as completely auxiliary to itself.[20]

The Woman's Foreign Missionary Society of the Methodist Protestant Church, organized by ladies in the Pittsburgh area in 1879, had its autonomy snatched from it in a highhanded manner. These women had been working through the Woman's Union Foreign Missionary Society, and they set up an independent organization which might collaborate with either the W.U.F.M.S. or the denominational Board of Foreign Missions whenever it should embark on an overseas program. This is an instance in which the women were ahead of the official denominational agencies. Soon, however, the constitution was changed, limiting cooperation to the church Board and placing the Society under the authority of the General Conference. The officers of the Board of Foreign Missions wanted the Society to be fully subordinate to it and all local monies to be paid directly into its treasury. The Board asked for a union of the two agencies, but the women declined. There was continued friction. The secretary of the Board aired the matter from the male point of view in the church magazine. Many ministers thereupon took offense at what they considered an aspect of the Women's Rights movement. An intersociety consultation appeared to improve matters for a short time, but many of the brethren were determined to get control of the women's funds and to deprive their Society of independence. The Society in 1884 petitioned the General Conference for recognition as an official board of the church; for continued control of its own funds while being under advisory supervision of the Board; for a clear division of program, with all work for

20 Estella H. Steinmetz, *Reminiscences, Being a Record of Five and Twenty Years' Progress in the Woman's Home and Foreign Missionary Society of the United Evangelical Church,* pp. 15-23.

women and children to be under the Society; and for freedom of its women missionaries to carry out their responsibilities in their own way. The Board followed this presentation with a statement of its own, ostensibly seconding the
women, but actually presenting seven "Rules for Governing
the Woman's Foreign Missionary Society of the Methodist
Protestant Church," being in effect a new constitution imposed on the women, and not of their own adoption. It took
all the initiative and power from the women, deprived them
of effective administration, and ended their appointment and
assignment of women missionaries. This statement had been
read to a committee of the women immediately before the
session, and, aghast at its implications, they yet had no chance
to challenge it. The chairman of the Committee on Missions prefaced his report with the statement that the women
had agreed to the proposal he was presenting! This prevented discussion, and the women, having no voice in the
meeting, could not even protest. They had to sit in silence
while the General Conference adopted a document — patently contrary to their own petition — which ended the independence of the Woman's Society and made it a servant
of the Board. It was an act of rank piracy, however justified
it may have been by contemporary ecclesiastical law and
theory.[21]

The early annals of the societies are filled with tales and
anecdotes of opposition. There are many stories of male jubi-
lation over supposed positive evidence of God's direct intervention to thwart the nefarious plans and pretensions of
the women. In the course of 1876-1877 *Advance* and *The
Congregationalist* engaged in an editorial duel over the
Woman's Boards. This exchange laid bare the widespread
masculine fear that this missionary effort primarily masked
the woman's suffrage and Woman's Rights movement. The
opponent declared: "The Cross of Christ is today prostituted
to the unholy work of degrading, coarsening the fine tone

---

[21] Mrs. M. A. Miller, *History of the Woman's Foreign Missionary
Society of the Methodist Protestant Church,* pp. 55-64.

of female character in our churches and in our country."
The spectacle of lady missionaries, officers, and executives of
the Boards addressing mixed audiences, speaking before the
assemblies of the American Board, and presiding over their
own meetings filled conservative males with horror. They
lamented the loss of Puritan womanhood. When the president of the W.B.M. of the Interior had to resign just before
the annual meeting of 1871, all older wives of ministers
refused the office because of the strong opposition of their
husbands, and a young wife had to dare to assume the post.
An eminent Methodist minister wrote in an editorial: "Some
of the most thoughtful minds are beginning to ask what is
to become of this Woman movement in the church." He ad-
vised: "Let them alone, — all through our history like move-
ments have started. Do not oppose them, and it will die out."

When Miss Isabella Thoburn came home on first furlough
her first invitation to speak at a Sunday service came from
a Presbyterian church, not one of her own Methodist churches.
She demurred; it was improper. The most she could do was
to sit in a front pew and answer any questions that might
be raised after the service. The questions came thick and
fast, and the answers developed into an effective address.
Thereafter, Miss Thoburn accepted invitations. It is amazing how long pulpits and platforms were closed to women
missionary spokesmen, but pulpits rapidly became available
to them compared with the floors of presbyteries, associations,
synods, conferences, and dioceses. As late as the 1930s one of
the oldest American churches still denied women a voice
before its general assembly. Miss Sue Weddell, the first woman
executive secretary for missionary education, was at first for-
bidden to make a report to the Synod of the Reformed
Church in America according to their policy. Happily the
fathers and brethren wanted to hear the report, and they
voted to waive that policy and permit her to speak. It may
comfort some persons to know that such antifeminine views
were not exclusively confined to the United States. When
Miss Weddell as co-executive secretary of the Foreign Missions Conference went to Great Britain as fraternal rep-

resentative to the Conference of Missionary Societies, she could not speak to the Baptists assembled in the Spurgeon Church until they voted to admit and hear her.

Once the societies had been established, men frequently endeavored to subordinate them and bring them under the control of the general boards or to absorb them. Sometimes it was by a power play, as in the case of the Methodist Protestants; sometimes it was through blandishments. Miss Frances J. Baker reports that one summer at Clifton Springs, in the course of a tea party after a mission program, Bishop Janes said that the scene was "poetic," and commended the Woman's Foreign Missionary Society of the Methodist Episcopal Church. "As the Parent Society and this were working together so harmoniously, and as the marital relation was the most sacred and delightful on earth, he proposed that the nuptials of the two be celebrated." The host declared that the Bishop had gone courting and must have his answer. Thereupon Mrs. Hibbard, as spokesman for the Woman's Society, replied that "she had been taught to be very honest in such matters, and she was now too old to change her habit in this particular. She confessed that she saw two insuperable obstacles to the match: the first was, they were *too near of kin* — the Bishop had just called one the Parent Society — and, secondly, there was *too great a disparity in their ages,* the one being fifty years older than the other." The Bishop declared that a courageous man was not to be daunted by one refusal.

The sheer weight of numbers and the power of the women's money soon had effect, but it was also the performance of the single women and the effectiveness of their work on the fields that won recognition and respect for the women's boards and societies. Nevertheless there was for decades grumbling by men that the women's work was built up to excessive proportions compared with the general program, that the women always had money for projects while the men had little or none, and that the women went their own independent way at home and abroad. Until the recent reorganization one often heard the remark by men that the

Woman's Division of Christian service ought to join the Methodist Church, and occasionally one still hears some Southern Baptist pastor assert that it is time for the Woman's Union to join the Convention.

During the short period of their existence through 1882 sixteen women's societies reported total receipts of $5,940,045, a colossal sum in relation to the purchasing power of the dollar today. Thirty-five agencies had a combined income of $1,412,235 in 1900. Income rose steadily. Receipts for 1923 as reported in the *World Missionary Atlas* of 1925 total $1,008,942 for eight Canadian women's societies and $8,987,577 for twenty-nine of the United States boards, five of which also reported giving $845,492 for home missions.[22]

Administrative costs were extremely low, salaries were meager, and almost all receipts were applied to support of workers and the erection and maintenance of institutions overseas. Some of the societies supported wives who were engaged in work for women and children, but the great majority sent out and supported unmarried women only. It is easily understood why the number of single women on the mission staff expanded so extensively. By 1882, for which year a general reporting was made, the few existing women's societies had sent forth and supported 694 unmarried missionaries, maintained hundreds of national workers, erected residences, schools, and hospitals, and had made women a major force in world mission. James S. Dennis, in his *Centennial Survey of Foreign Missions,* reports in 1900, serving under all United States boards, 1,291 wives, 1,015 single women, and 113 women physicians who might be either. The Canadian boards at that time listed 44 wives, 50 single women, and 9 women physicians. It is interesting to discover that of these women 389 wives, 856 single women and wid-

---

[22] Statistics in this and following paragraphs are derived from the following: Daggett, *op. cit.,* for 1882; James S. Dennis, *Centennial Survey of Foreign Missions;* Harlan P. Beach, *A Geography and Atlas of Protestant Missions,* II; same, 1906; Dennis, Beach, and Fahs, *World Atlas of Christian Missions;* Harlan P. Beach and Charles H. Fahs, *World Missionary Atlas.*

ows, and 96 physicians were being supported by women's societies in the United States, and 46 single women and 8 physicians by the Canadian ladies' boards. Harlan P. Beach, using a different classification of societies, gives somewhat different figures for the same year: 1,817 wives and 1,646 single women under the North American agencies. The next decade saw a steady increase, and the statistics reported for 1910 are: married women not physicians 2,548; unmarried women 2,122, and women physicians 180 — for all North American boards. The figures for the North American women's societies given in the *World Missionary Atlas* of 1925 for 1923 add up to 4,401 wives overseas and 260 more working with Indians and Orientals in North America, or a total of 4,661; and 4,328 single women abroad plus 496 working under the same boards in North America, or a total of 4,824.

There was a similar increase in the commissioning of single women and widows by the societies in the United Kingdom and other sending countries, although the number of new women's societies was by no means as great as in North America. The Church Missionary Society, for example, in 1873 had on its roll only eleven single women; in 1883, fifteen; but in 1893 there were 134, and the next year the figure jumped to 160. The following table indicates the rise in the number of single women and widows.

Year	All Missionaries	All Men	Wives	N.A. Wives	Unmarried Women	N.A. Single Women	Women Physicians	N.A. Women Physicians
1900	18,782	10,214	4,340	1,291	3,628	1,015	223	113
1910	21,307	9,788	5,934	2,548	5,377	2,122	348	180
1923	29,188	11,444	8,619	4,661	9,125	4,824		

The extensive employment of single women and widows radically changed the proportion of the sexes in the missionary staff. When William G. Lennox made a study of the health and turnover of missionaries serving under the boards of six United States denominations through 1929, he summarized the trend as follows:

Of the total years which missionaries of these six boards have served, three fifths belonged to women, two fifths to men. In the course of the century there has been a remarkable increase in the number of women workers as compared with the increase of men. In 1830, like animals entering the Ark, missionaries went to the field in pairs: for each man on the field there was nearly one woman. In 1880, for each man there were one and one-third women; in 1929, for each man there were 2.02 women. Expressed in percentages, the missionary personnel was female to the extent of 49 per cent in 1830, 57 per cent in 1880, and 67 per cent in 1929.[23]

The above table indicates that the same situation prevailed in the entire staff engaged in the foreign mission. In 1925 the statistics show that 60.8 percent of the missionaries were women.

It should be noted that the nondenominational mission societies, which proliferated in the same period when the women's societies arose, employed single women from the very beginning of their activities, but for a long time most of them were British and any North American women serving in them are reported in British listings. Dr. J. Hudson Taylor at the Centenary Conference stated that serving under the China Inland Mission in 1882 were fifty-six wives and ninety-five single women. The first two North American societies appear in the 1900 listing by Dennis: the Central America Mission with eight wives and ten single women, and the American Ramabai Association with one wife and four single women.

The new recognition given the woman missionary, her special society, and her work for women and children is revealed in the reports of the great popular interdenominational and international missionary conferences. There were no women members of the Conference on Missions held at Liverpool in 1860, and the work got only passing mention. The Rev. John Fordyce gave a brief address on "Female Education in the East" at one of the evening "soirées" — not

---

[23] William G. Lennox, *The Health and Turnover of Missionaries* (N. Y.: Foreign Missions Conf. of N. A., 1933), p. 28.

at a regular session. Two India missionaries and Dr. Lockhart of China, discussing "native agents," advocated employing native female missionaries, and a minute on the subject stated that "the power of female Christian influence should be employed as far as practicable." Quite in contrast with Liverpool, however, the Centenary Conference on Protestant Missions of the World at London in 1888, fully recognized the place special women's work had won in the enterprise, and women participated in their own right. Among the members were 345 women from Great Britain and Ireland, thirty-two from the United States, and four from Canada. There was none from the Continent of Europe or the British colonies. The American women were especially vocal. One session on special work was devoted to "Women's Mission to Women"; and there were two sessions of a sectional meeting on "Woman's Work in the Mission Field," when four papers were presented followed by lively comment and discussion. Miss Abbie B. Child of the Woman's Board of Missions, Congregational, ended her address with the assertion that work for women had increased fully fivefold in the past twenty years, and could at that moment be doubled again if the women were to enter the places waiting for them and there were means to send them. Men from India and China bore testimony to the worth of this ministry, and the aged African Bishop Samuel A. Crowther of the Niger commended it. A lone male voice, that of the General Superintendent of the American Free Methodist Church, proclaimed, "Let the women preach as well as labor in an inferior position."[24]

The Columbian Exposition at Chicago in 1893 was notable for the Parliament of Religions held in connection with it. There was also among the related conferences a "Woman's Congress of Missions," which gave recognition to the importance and power of Christian women in the world mission

---

[24] *Conference on Missions Held in 1860 at Liverpool* (London: James Nesbit, 1860), pp. 112, 148, 205, 224, 239, 273-274; *Report of the Centenary Conference on Protestant Missions of the World, Held in Exeter Hall (June 9th-19th), London, 1888*, ed. Rev. James Johnston, 2 vols. (N. Y.: Revell, 1888), I, 398-414, II, 140-183.

and in intercultural contacts. This Congress was in session three days, and it was organized and convened by a committee of women with Mrs. Franklin W. Fisk of Chicago as chairman. The chairman, when opening the Congress, said:

> It has been said that "the spirit of Missions is not simply a phase of Christianity — it is Christianity"; and also that the crowning glory of the nineteenth century is the great work that woman is doing for the elevation of her own sex. Accepting these propositions as true, it is upon this two-fold basis we rest our claim, and submit the question whether this Woman's Congress of Missions should not be considered preeminent in importance, and demand the very highest consideration and effort.

Mrs. Benjamin Douglas declared the motive of all women's work to be "Glory to God, goodwill to man." Papers were read on "Women and the World's Religions," several on the history of British women's missions, and one on American women's boards. Others followed on Deaconesses, "Women and Medical Missions," and "Women and Education in Missions." In the concluding address, Mrs. A. F. Schauffler asserted that women's missionary work is a power for good in four ways: in diffusing missionary information and forging a sympathetic personal link with workers in the fields, in planning and carrying on specific work for women and children, in promoting systematic giving in the churches, and in training the young to an intelligent interest in missions. A report on the Congress was published entitled, *Women in Missions.*[25]

Popular acclaim of the women's missionary movement reached its highest peak at the Ecumenical Missionary Conference, New York, 1900. The Report states:

> Women's work was recognized as never before. At the previous conferences held in England woman's work had some recognition, and a number of delegates attended the London Conference of 1888, but women were never in evidence as

---

[25] *Women in Missions. Papers and Addresses presented at the Woman's Congress of Missions, October 2-4, 1893, in the Hall of Columbus, Chicago,* compiled by Rev. E. M. Whery (N. Y.: American Tract Soc., 1894).

they were at these meetings; they took part in the discussions, and read papers, besides holding ten sectional meetings on the various phases of woman's work. The crowds that thronged the churches where these meetings were held were so great that at some of them it was found necessary to lock the doors, while an immense number were turned away, and an overflow meeting was organized in Calvary Baptist Church, with Mrs. Charles P. Thorpe, of Philadelphia, presiding, and a number of missionaries speaking. The enthusiasm was contagious, and as one woman said: "If any man has had lurking in his heart any objections to woman's work, they must melt away before the impressive demonstration of these woman's meetings!"[26]

No, it was no longer possible for men to deny women participation in world mission, which they had so patently earned. They simply asked that the women keep their proper place. As the secretary of the American Baptist Missionary Union well expressed prevailing sentiment at the Centenary Conference:

While it must be accepted as the duty of single ladies to be helpful in all departments of the work, it ought to be expected of them that they will carefully abstain from any interference with matters not specially committed to their hands. Woman's work in the foreign field must be careful to recognize the headship of man in ordering the affairs of the kingdom of God. We must not allow the major vote of the better sex, nor the ability and efficiency of so many of our female helpers, nor even the exceptional faculty for leadership and organization which some of them have displayed in their work, to discredit the natural and predestined head-

---

[26] *Report of the Ecumenical Missionary Conference, New York, 1900,* I, 46. There were no women among the vice-presidents, the General Committee, or the Finance Committee, and Miss Abbie B. Child was the only lady member of the Executive Committee; but women were on many committees and predominated in those on such things as "Free Entertainment" and "Serving Tea"! Women's work was generally treated under each topic and thus well integrated, but there were special meetings on "Woman's Work in Foreign Missions," a mass meeting for women in Carnegie Hall, and an evening meeting on women's work in the same place.

ship of man in Missions, as well as in the Church of God: "Adam was first formed, then Eve," and "the head of the woman is the man." This order of creation has not been changed by Redemption, and we must conform all our plans and policies for the uplifting of the race through the power of the Gospel to this Divine ordinance.[27]

---

[27] *Report of the Centenary Conference of Protestant Missions, 1888,* II, 167, 168.

V

WOMEN'S WORK FOR WOMEN
AND CHILDREN

MALE COMMENTATORS ON THE WOMEN'S MISSIONARY MOVEMENT
were apt to remind the ladies that although the size of the
enterprise had increased enormously there was nothing really
new about the program being carried forward. Everything
being done by the single women, they said, had either been
done regularly or had been attempted earlier by the wives
and even the men. This was essentially true, but none of
these things had ever before been done so extensively, intensively, and continuously. Miss Rainy of the Free Church of
Scotland at the Centenary Conference had listed the mani-
fold types of activity being carried on by women: teaching
in day, Sunday, and industrial schools; maintenance of orphanages and boarding schools; the zenana mission or house-
to-house visitation in India and China; evangelistic work
among the poor in villages and country districts, at fairs and
and sacred places, in hospitals and prisons; Bible classes and

117

mothers' meetings for converts; the training and supervision of native Christian agents; the preparation of vernacular literature; and last, but not least, medical work among women and children, now in its infancy, but possessing infinite possibilities. To that list would soon be added higher education for women. The medical work and the higher education for girls were actually quite different than anything that had been previously undertaken.

Even in evangelism, pioneer work, which had been so unique and unbelievable when Eleanor Macomber had done it, was now extensively undertaken by women. Hudson Taylor in the 1888 Conference reported that the China Inland Mission had many inland stations manned only by ladies with the assistance of native workers. The Baptist secretary, who wanted women to keep their proper place under male domination, enthusiastically described the activity of Mrs. Murilla B. Ingalls, who appears to have violated his cardinal rule. She had continued in service after the death of her husband, Lovell, and singlehanded founded and supervised the Thonzé station in Burma, where the church became numerous and prosperous. She satisfied the secretary's scruples by refraining from public addresses and ecclesiastical functions. But she was the power behind the whole enterprise. Mrs. Ingalls, it was stated, taught both the men and women in everything that concerns Christian truth and church organization. She selected, trained, directed, and encouraged the men in evangelistic service. "She guides the church in the appointment of its pastor, instructs him in Bible truth, pastoral theology, including homiletical training, and supervises all the work of the station." She directed the central school, selected candidates for teaching, guided them, and sent them to village schools. The missionary organized *zayat* preaching, organized also a circulating library, and established a widespread system of Bible and tract distribution. Her perfect mastery of self, good judgment, calm temper, firmness joined with kindness, tact, and Christian spirit overcame occasional opposition. Her greatest difficulty arose from her refusal to perform baptisms and marriages. Dr. Murdock overcame his wish that

Mrs. Ingalls were a man and prayed for both men and women like her.[1]

Most early evangelistic work not connected with schools, hospitals, and dispensaries was of two types, the zenana mission to the secluded women of the upper classes in Asia and the more open, public contact with the poor of the cities and of the country villages. The mission to the women of the well-to-do and socially elite families could not hope to reach large numbers, and some missions did not favor it for that reason. Others took a long-range point of view. While limited, affecting relatively few individuals, and time consuming, it relied upon the power of women in even the most restricted and traditional society. Through their influence with husbands and sons change could be induced in society and through their daughters sent to school the elevation of women could more directly be undertaken. This long-range aim by no means detracted from the personal concern for individuals. The missionaries who gained access to the homes of well-to-do families taught the women English and Bible, instructed in sewing and embroidery, conversed and read with them, answered their questions about life in Europe and America, and imparted practical information about health and hygiene, diet, and child care. They sought friendship, and through friendship to introduce their Lord and Savior. After the turn of the century some of the missionaries introduced the "zenana party," inviting their acquaintances to the mission compound for conversation, music, an illustrated talk, and food. On these occasions great pains were taken to safeguard all the proprieties so that the antagonism of husbands be not aroused. Such a party was for many a woman the first taste of freedom and of contact with modernity. A cultural revolution has swept away female segregation and seclusion, except in extremely conservative quarters. In the country where zenana work began there has been a woman Prime Minister of the nation. The

---

[1] *Report of the Centenary Conference on Protestant Missions of the World, 1888,* II, 164; see also Annie R. Gracey, *op. cit.,* pp. 196-201.

women of Africa and Asia have found freedom and influence in professions, business, homes, and politics. The work of the women missionaries was no small factor in initiating this colossal change. Not the least important effect of zenana visitation was to bring girls into mission schools and under the influence of Western Christian teaching.

Village women of the lower castes and classes were far less restricted and more open to approach. Village itineration was arduous, but the lady missionaries regularly undertook it, except in the most difficult seasons, and at those times they would concentrate on work at their stations. Miss A. E. Baskerville˙of the Canadian Baptists described the typical approach to women in an Indian village.[2] A missionary accompanied by one or two Bible women would lodge in a central chapel or school for some weeks in the area to be itinerated, or in some regions a houseboat could be used, or a tent would be set up at some village for a few days and then moved to another. If operating from a central location, the women would walk to surrounding villages, devoting a few days to each. During the morning village women would be encountered on the streets and at the well. They would ask the visitors the usual questions: Where did they come from? How old were they? Were they married? Why not? Why had they come? And that last question opened an opportunity for serious conversation. At noon there would be a children's gathering at the tent or lodging place, followed by a mothers' meeting or a gathering of women already Christian. The remainder of the afternoon would be devoted to visiting women in their homes. At night there would be a Bible class. This initial approach would be followed up intensively by the Bible women in the weeks to come, and the missionary would return from time to time.

Accepting the teaching of Henry Venn in England and Rufus Anderson in the United States, missionaries generally sought to foster the growth of churches under their own

---

[2] *Report of the Ecumenical Missionary Conference, New York, 1900*, II, 94-96.

pastors and to nourish them to independence, self-support, and evangelistic activity. Not only national pastors, but "native workers" of all sorts were recruited, trained, and employed. This staff was called "the native agency." The women missionaries were responsible for the female portion of this company — the Bible women, female teachers, medical workers, matrons, and the like. Each woman evangelist knew the limitations of her own personal effort and sought to multiply its effect through the Bible women whom she trained and directed. The Bible woman, catechist or evangelist, was the lowliest employee on the hierarchical ladder of the mission churches, but usually devoted, faithful, and energetic. In newly opened areas the missionaries would personally instruct their recruits individually and often in extremely elementary fashion. But special training schools rapidly developed. China in 1900 may be taken as an example. There were the Charlotte Duryee Training School at Amoy with forty-seven students; the Wesleyan Training School for Women at Canton with forty-eight; the English Presbyterian Training School at Chinchiu with twenty-four; at Foochow the American Board, Methodist Episcopal, and Church Missionary Society schools with twenty-eight, twenty-eight, and twenty-four respectively; and thirty-four other schools scattered throughout the land. There were at that time more than thirty such schools training Bible women in India. Throughout all the missions in all lands in that year there were 3,513 women enrolled in the training schools.

The length of the course varied considerably. Always there were certain essentials in the curriculum, Bible study being the primary emphasis with special attention to the life of Christ. Simple Theology, a little Church History, and a bit of Geography were usually considered important, as were also Physiology, Hygiene, and Child Care. Singing and the playing of a simple instrument for accompanying singing would be part of the program. Elementary Astronomy, intended to deal with astrology, might be taught. And, of course, there was much emphasis on methods of work and techniques — itineration, house visitation, "tent work," story telling, Bible teaching, Sunday schools, women's meetings, sewing classes, and children's meetings.

The quality of the Bible women varied considerably. Some of these women, working on a bare subsistence wage, were employed to keep them alive when cast out by their families after conversion. Others were extremely able and effective agents, highly motivated and dedicated to their ministry. Much of the effectiveness of their work depended upon the ability of the missionaries to train, direct, and inspire them. They were the shock troops of the women's movement in the invasion of the female masses. The quality of both the Bible women and their training continued to rise through the decades. At first only middle-aged women were employed, but as a pool of educated girls became available for recruiting the age level dropped. Gradually there came to be established training schools which could require considerable education as prerequisite for admission and which could maintain professional standards, such as the union Bible Teachers Training School for Young Women in Nanking, and the Harris and Ellinwood Schools in Manila.

The educational program of the missions similarly responded to the tremendous increase in the number of women missionaries. Day schools jumped from a few hundred to 23,723 with 1,073,205 pupils in 1900. In 1910 there were 30,185 elementary and village schools with 2,165,842 pupils, and 742 kindergartens with 27,005 children enrolled. The kindergartens were an important innovation, particularly in Japan, and were potent means of reaching mothers. Boarding schools, especially on the high school level, and normal schools received particular attention, not only for the education of girls and the transformation of their life but for the training of teachers for the vast system of day schools. Dennis' *Centennial Survey* reported 43,714 girls enrolled in those institutions. The 1910 statistics listed 41,313 girls in the high schools; and in 1923 the number was 55,154 in the high schools and 3,112 in the teacher training schools. Higher education of women was usually developed through interdenominational cooperation and will be treated in the next chapter. Not only the number of schools and pupils increased dramatically, but the quality was greatly improved. Isabella Thoburn and Laura Haygood may be taken as typical examples of missionaries engaged in this work.

Isabella Thoburn's thirty-one years of ministry at Lucknow, India, illustrates how education for girls could develop naturally and extensively under a woman who was an inspiring teacher, a true friend to her students, and an able administrator. She was the very first missionary appointed by the Woman's Foreign Missionary Society of the Methodist Episcopal Church, and the Society had to borrow money to make the appointment. Miss Thoburn's vocation to service in India came through the appeal of her brother, James Mills Thoburn, later Bishop, who had become convinced that education of girls was essential to the progress of Christianity and the development of the church in India. He was also convinced that the experienced and able young teacher in Ohio who was his sister was the person to inaugurate this work for the Methodist Church. Having arrived in India in January, 1870, the new missionary opened her first school in April in a rented room in the bazaar in Lucknow, with six little Christian girls, and a man with a club outside the door to protect them. A few weeks later the school moved to a missionary bungalow, and thence to a rented house as the number of pupils increased to twenty-five. The following year the Mission was able to purchase from a Muslim gentleman an estate of nine acres with a large house and beautiful flower gardens, named Lal Bagh or the Ruby Garden.

Miss Thoburn during the first years established a number of other schools and supervised them. She trained Bible women, and engaged in other work. But soon the expanding school at Lal Bagh demanded her full time. The acquisition of this property made a boarding school possible, and it was to be of a higher quality than any previous one. Local day pupils were also admitted, and in 1892 there were ninety-six boarders and sixty-four day pupils. As dormitories were erected the number accommodated was increased.

Miss Jennie Tinsley arrived to join Miss Thoburn in 1871, and through successive years other notable teachers came to the school. The curriculum had to provide for the full range of classes from the beginning through high school, for the pupils ranged from six years to young adulthood. There was no segregation by class or caste, and life in this community was a foretaste of a new kind of society.

Achievement in one field eventually would lead to demands in a new one. By 1887, when substantial additional funds were invested in the enterprise, it was determined to stress quality secondary education, and the name was changed to Girls' High School. Many of the graduates became teachers, Bible women, and pastors' wives. As homemakers others set a powerful example for relatives and neighbors. Good secondary education produced a desire for higher education, and there was then no Christian college for women. Miss Thoburn was forced to become a pioneer in that field. The collegiate department was created in 1887, with Miss Hester V. Monsell as principal, and with three students enrolled. Invalided home for five years from 1887 to 1892, Miss Thoburn raised funds for the new work and organized continuing special support. Equipment and library were gradually added, and the staff was augmented by qualified teachers. The quality of work was so good that affiliation with Calcutta University was granted, including the right to prepare for its degrees. Miss Thoburn attended the Ecumenical Missionary Conference in New York in 1900 and there made a powerful plea for higher education for women. Soon she returned to India, but quickly succumbed to cholera on September 1, 1901. The institution was named in her honor Isabella Thoburn College, and continues its eminence in the field of higher education for women.[3]

Colleges could not develop until high-quality high schools in sufficient number made them necessary, and such high schools were for a long time the principal key to the advance-

---

[3] Helen B. Montgomery, *Western Women in Eastern Lands*, pp. 166-176; Frances J. Baker, *The Story of the Woman's Foreign Missionary Society of the Methodist Episcopal Church*, pp. 179-194.

ment of women in society and in the church. Laura Askew Haygood was one of the most influential educators in this field in China. She was born October 14, 1845, at Watkinsville, Georgia, but from the age of seven lived in Atlanta, where her mother conducted a school with both primary and high school departments. Her brother, Atticus, was a bishop in the Methodist Episcopal Church, South. After a conversion experience, Laura joined Trinity Methodist Church in Atlanta in 1858. She was educated so well in her mother's school that she was able to graduate from Wesleyan Female College in 1864 after only two years there. After teaching for a year at Palmer Institute at Oxford, she returned to Atlanta following the end of the Civil War and took charge of the primary department of her mother's school. When the city of Atlanta opened its Girls' High School in 1872, she became a teacher there, and in 1877 was appointed principal. During all her career at Girls' High School Miss Haygood also taught Atlanta's "normal class" or teacher training course, and came to exert great influence among the city's teachers. She was an extremely gifted teacher of teachers. Putting this talent to the service of the church, she taught a normal class for Sunday school teachers of several denominations every Saturday. Not content with administration, she taught English, Latin, Moral Science, and Mental Philosophy in the high school and a class of older girls at Trinity Church. She and her pupils organized three Sunday schools which grew into churches, and she was organizer and president of a home mission society which conducted an industrial school.

Miss Haygood corresponded with friends among the missionaries in China, but her own sense of a personal vocation to service in that country came through an appeal by Dr. Young J. Allen, superintendent of the China Mission, for an experienced and capable educator to develop the work for women and children in the Shanghai region. He asked Miss Haygood's help in finding the right person, but his appeal came to her as the very calling of the Holy Spirit to her personally. She made her decision in February, 1884, and when the Woman's Board of Foreign Missions of the M. E. Church, South, met in June, the appointment of an educator of such stature and fame was enthusiastically hailed. This is truly remarkable in view of the fact that Miss Haygood was often in very bad health, having been bothered by sciatica for many years and for some years having had to walk with crutches.

A woman of such high stature and broad experience could not hope to devote herself to teaching alone, and just as soon as she arrived in Shanghai on November 17, 1884, Miss Haygood found herself in charge of all the work of the Woman's Board in Shanghai and the surrounding country. While engaged in language study and all that heavy responsibility, she especially devoted herself to the Clopton boarding school for girls and to two day schools. At Clopton she stressed teacher training, later merging it with Mary Lambuth School at Soochow. She deemed it wise to consolidate and concentrate existing day schools at Trinity and Moore Memorial Churches, and built up the two centralized schools in quality and numbers. The curriculum consisted of Chinese Classics, various Western subjects such as Arithmetic and Geography, and Christian Teaching. When these two schools were sufficiently well grounded, Miss Haygood established clusters of day schools around these strong centers. There was still much opposition locally to the education of girls, but through the efforts of the superintendent it came about that two-thirds of the pupils in these schools were girls. The preparation of teachers being a veritable passion with her, she conducted a teacher training class every week and through it impressed her spirit and standards on her teachers. Somehow she also found time to teach elementary English to boys in the Anglo-Chinese College, to teach a Bible class for foreign women in Shanghai, and to teach still another for sailors. She did much evangelistic house-to-house visitation, and supervised other aspects of the women's work in the district. This half-crippled woman was a giant of a person. All this while, however, Miss Haygood's chief objective, in which she had the support of Dr.

Allen, was the creation of a high school for girls which would match in quality the Anglo-Chinese College for boys.

Having come to China in maturity and after much administrative experience, Laura Haygood gained early an understanding of the problems of adjustment demanded of new women missionaries. Therefore, when she opened the high school for girls she added to it a home and training school for new missionaries where they might for two years study the Chinese language and culture and be introduced to the work of the church. Miss Haygood, with the consent of the Board, raised the needed funds for the school and home by forming a joint stock company with shares valued at ten dollars each. Her circular letter of 1885 to the women of the M. E. Church, South, stimulated tremendous enthusiasm. The money came. Land was bought in 1886, building begun in 1889, and the plant completed in 1891. Meanwhile Miss Haygood became extremely ill, sought relief in North China and Japan, but still far from well returned to her post because so many of her missionary colleagues had been taken by death. The school and home, named McTyeire in honor of a bishop, officially opened on March 16, 1892. Beginning with an enrollment of nine pupils, the student body expanded so rapidly that in 1900 another building was added. Seventy-five boarders and twenty-five day students could be accommodated. Pupils were of two kinds, daughters of the wealthy non-Christian gentry and officialdom and Christian girls of families in very moderate circumstances. The first class graduated in 1900. McTyeire became the foremost private girls' high school in the Shanghai area, and maintained that position until expropriated by the Communist regime.

Versatility and a readiness to accept new responsibilities, even when conflicting with one's own dearest wishes, were ever demanded of the woman missionary. Given her ability and experience, it is not surprising that when Laura Haygood returned to China after furlough in 1896 she came as director of all the work of the Woman's Board. This included supervision of Shanghai, Nantziang, Kading, Soochow, and Sungkiang. If women's work was to be developed, the administration of it must be provided. Miss Haygood gave new stimulation to evangelism by establishing two schools for Bible women at Soochow and Sungkiang. Itineration among the stations took a heavy toll of her strength, and she became chronically ill in the summer of 1899. After she had been confined to her room in the McTyeire Home for seven months, Laura Haygood died on April 29, 1900. But her work lived after her in McTyeire High School, in the memorial Laura A. Haygood Home and School at Soochow, and in the lives of her students and the workers whom she had trained and directed. Moreover, through her writings and correspondence she had come to hold a place in the Southern Methodist Church very similar to that of Lottie Moon among the Southern Baptists, and innumerable memorial services were held in the United States.[4]

Industrial schools were at the far end of the educational spectrum from high-quality high schools and colleges, and these nonacademic institutions attempted to give girls and women a practical trade by which to support themselves or supplement the family income. They got relatively little attention compared with the academic institutions, but made a needed contribution. Dennis' report of 1900 lists for the whole worldwide mission only twenty-four such institutions for girls and twenty-six that admitted both sexes. They taught girls spinning, weaving, sewing, skilled needlework, lacemaking, laundering, cooking, baking, dairying, basketmaking, gardening, dressmaking, shoemaking, mat-weaving, and other crafts. Some grew into substantial industries, such as the lacemaking business in the Nagercoil, South India, area, sponsored by the London Missionary Society. However, Americans did little of this. The Southern Presbyterians taught embroidery, silk-winding, and dressmaking at Hangchow, and the Lutherans embroidery at Guntur, India. The Cum-

4 Oswald E. and Anna M. Brown, *Life and Letters of Laura Askew Haygood* (Nashville: Publishing House of the M. E. Church, South, 1904).

berland Presbyterians taught sewing, drawnwork, and house-keeping in a school in Mexico. Only in Japan were Americans, including the Canadians, notably involved in such schools, where there were nine schools for girls and a tenth that also admitted boys. Industrial work was more likely to be part of the management of American orphanages, where the object was to make the boys and girls self-supporting as adults and sometimes to raise funds for the institution. We find reported in some orphanages spinning, weaving, dairying, embroidery, rope-making, and one instance of the manufacturing of wire-spring mattresses. One orphanage specialized in training girls to be *ayahs* or caretakers of children, cooks, and practical nurses.

Orphanages never assumed in Protestant missions the high place accorded them in Roman Catholic missions as a major resource for building the church. The Chinese practice of exposing girl babies to die after birth, wrung the hearts of the missionaries, but American women had established only seven orphanages for girls there by 1900. Elsewhere floods, famines, earthquakes, wars, and persecutions left thousands of children orphaned or forever separated from their families. There were two instances of famines in India when two missions alone rescued 700 children in one case and 750 in another. There were a half-dozen American orphanages in all of Africa, but scores of them in India. The American Board and its associated Women's Boards maintained twelve orphanages in the Turkish Empire at that time. An investigation was made in 1895 of the records of 130 women who as girls had been victims of the Indian famine of 1860 and placed in an orphanage at that time. After thirty-five years eight were then physicians, five hospital assistants, twenty-eight school teachers, fourteen were wives of pastors and themselves employed in church work, and thirty-two were volunteer teachers or church workers. That same orphanage in twenty-four years had sent out of its community 180 Christian workers.[5]

---

[5] Montgomery, *op. cit.*, pp. 140-141.

Ministries of compassion, usually called philanthropic agencies in the reports, were on the whole minimal, largely because preoccupation with evangelism, education, and medicine for the masses and the elite made most boards and societies reluctant to invest personnel and funds in forms of service to limited numbers, bringing small statistical returns. Originally lepers were approached purely as a philanthropic service because little was known about the cure and care of the malady; and, while various missions might engage in maintenance of "leper asylums," the support came largely from special missions to lepers. The Presbyterians had a leprosarium for women at Saheranpur, India. Blind and deaf-mutes were cared for from a similar point of view. With advance in the medical care of leprosy, the work with lepers was transferred from "philanthropy" to medicine, but the blind and others long remained the objects of charity and of compassion for those essentially hopeless. The Presbyterians established a home and school for the blind in Canton in 1887 and a school for deaf-mutes in Chefoo the next year. The Episcopalians opened an institution for the blind in Shanghai as early as 1857. The Reformed Church operated a school and home for rescued slaves at Muscat, dating from 1896. Opium refuges in China seem to have been the responsibility of the general boards, not of the women. The Woman's Union Foreign Missionary Society maintained "converts' homes" in Shanghai and at Calcutta and Cawnpore. The Congregationalists had homes for widows at Ahmednagar and Bombay; the Free Methodists at Balasore; and the Methodist Episcopal women at Kolar, Lodipur, Lucknow, Pakur, Shahjehanpur, Pithoragarh, and Calcutta. The Methodists also conducted a Home for Destitute Women and Girls at Penang, Malaysia, an Old Folk's Home and Orphanage at Nagoya, Japan, and rescue centers for girls at Nagasaki and Miyazaki. All of these existed before 1900. From 1900 to 1910 there was some augmentation of the philanthropic agencies, but after 1910 they tended to decrease. A small number of American women gave heroic and devoted service in these institutions while European missionaries had a

more voluminous record, but there has been little or no celebration of their work. "Philanthropy" attracted neither the
personnel nor the money that went into work producing
more spectacular success.

Only medicine received attention and support equal to
that given evangelism and education. The entrance of women
into this field of work stimulated it generally more than
the others, and henceforth it formed the third major department of work in most missions.

When the first American woman's board was founded in
1861 the most famous living missionary was a physician,
David Livingstone. But his fame was due not to medical
service, but to his explorations of central Africa. There was
then but a small company of missionary doctors, and their
status was that of "assistant missionary," just the same as
the women. Only eight hospitals and dispensaries were in
existence, and that reveals the minor place accorded the
ministry of health and healing in the missionary enterprise
of that day. Doctors had been sent by the boards and societies primarily to care for the health of the missionary
families, but they could not leave healing hands off the dis-
eased, ailing, injured masses all around them. It was soon
discovered that their service created a climate favorable to
the mission, and gradually the physician was recognized as
having a genuine place in the enterprise. Some missionaries,
following the example of Peter Parker of Canton, earned
both theological and medical degrees before going to the
field. Yet it was not until women doctors invaded the field
in force that medicine began to be regarded as an essential
Christian ministry and a legitimate mode of proclamation
of the gospel of the Great Physician. The emphasis that
the women's boards put on medicine stimulated the general
church boards to lay greater stress on the healing ministry.
The American Board advanced the doctors from "assistant"
to "missionary" in 1897.

The scanty company of missionary doctors, probably much
less than one hundred in 1860, had increased to 711, including 222 women, by 1900. Of the women physicians 129

were North Americans. In 1910 there were 667 men and 348 women physicians serving under all missionary agencies. Nineteen hospitals and dispensaries were established in the decade of the 1860s, 33 in the 1870s, 119 in the 1880s, and 341 in the 1890s. The 1910 statistics report 576 hospitals and 1077 dispensaries. A very large part of this new, huge volume of service was care of women and children. Men physicians had not been without such patients. Peter Parker's first patient was a woman, and women and children came to his hospital in crowds. But even in China relatively few women would permit examination and care by a male physician, and it was entirely impossible in the case of the sequestered women of India and Muslim countries. The health plight of Eastern women (little seems to have been said about Africans) lay heavily on the hearts and consciences of Western Christian women. Consequently medicine was from the outset stressed by the women's boards, and they built up the service as rapidly as women physicians could be recruited. This was in many ways the greatest single new development in women's work.

A remarkable woman, Mrs. Sarah J. Hale, editor of *Godey's Lady's Book*, had endeavored to rally the American women to this cause by founding a Ladies' Medical Missionary Society in Philadelphia in 1851. However, she was attacked and ridiculed unmercifully. And there were no women physicians. But by the time that the women's foreign missions boards and societies came to be organized, the Woman's College of Medicine of Philadelphia had weathered the antagonism of the medical profession and the general public and was graduating women doctors.

It was recognized from the very beginning that even thousands of Western women doctors could not begin to meet the health needs of the female populace of Oriental and African lands. Teaching as well as medical practice would be required of the missionaries. Medicine is today perhaps the most prestige-giving profession open to Indian women, and there are thousands of women doctors in that land. It all began in that country with a women's medical class opened May 1, 1869, at Naini Tal by the clergyman-physician, Dr. Humphrey, of the Methodist Episcopal Mission. He had been approached by an enlightened gentleman, Nund Kishon, with the request to undertake the education of a few women in midwifery and treatment of diseases of women and children. He proposed to find half the expenses himself and to apply to the Colonial government for the remainder. The application was made, but the governor met so much opposition from doctors that he could not grant it. Nevertheless, Sir William Muir considered the project so important and promising that he gave the money out of his own pocket. At the end of two years the four young women of Dr. Humphrey's class stood a rigorous examination and were granted certificates to practice. Meanwhile, Mrs. Thomas of the Methodist Mission at Bareilly, who supervised an orphanage, like many another missionary wife treated minor ailments and longed for the presence of a fully qualified woman physician. She began preparing a class of senior girls in the orphanage for entrance into a medical class when there might be one. She further appealed to her former colleague, Mrs. Annie R. Gracey, now in Philadelphia to try to interest the Woman's Union Foreign Missionary Society in sending out the highly desired doctor. That Society was favorable. Mrs. Gracey then turned to the Woman's Medical College in the city in search of the right person. Clara A. Swain, then about to receive the M.D. degree, was recommended. By the time she gave her assent, the Methodist Episcopal Woman's Foreign Missionary Society had been organized. The Union Society gave up its claim on the young doctor, and she was appointed by her own Methodist sisters. Along with Miss Isabella Thoburn she sailed for India on November 3, 1869, the very first woman medical missionary appointed to any field by any society or board.[6]

Born in Elmira, Clara Swain grew up in Castile, New

---

[6] *Ibid.*, pp. 127-129; Annie R. Gracey, "Woman's Medical Work in Missions," *Women in Missions: Papers and Addresses presented at the Woman's Congress of Missions, 1893, Chicago*, pp. 156-174; Frances J. Baker, *op. cit.*, pp. 118-120.

York. After a period of teaching school, her interest in medicine led her to take a position in the Castile Sanitarium, where she could study under Dr. Cordelia A. Greene while working. After three years she was admitted to the Woman's Medical College in Philadelphia. She accepted the call to missionary service upon graduation. Arriving at Bareilly in January, 1870, Dr. Swain plunged into her work. Her first year's report recorded 1,225 patients treated at the mission house and 250 home visits, some of them to zenanas. During the second year she was called into twenty-six more homes of secluded women. In March, 1870, she began teaching the class of fourteen orphan young women whom Mrs. Thomas had prepared. This class graduated April 10, 1873, and certificates were granted permitting them to practice.[7]

A hospital with a dispensary was a crying need. The property desired for that institution belonged to the Nawab of Rampur. When Miss Swain asked him if he would sell the house and a portion of land, the prince astounded and delighted her by giving her outright all forty acres. The mansion was remodeled and equipped, and a dispensary built. The latter opened in 1873 and the hospital in 1874. Later this institution was given Miss Swain's name. Patients in the tenth year numbered more than seven thousand. Dr. Swain's fame spread throughout the land.

The statistics of this and other women's hospitals and dispensaries superficially make it appear as if once a doctor had arrived on the scene and a hospital opened crowds rushed through its doors. But the physicians found it quite otherwise. Miss A. K. Marsten said at the Centenary Conference: "It is quite a mistake to suppose that Indian women are debarred from medical treatment altogether. From our point of view they are certainly debarred from sufficient and effectual medical aid; but from their own point of view they

---

7 Mrs. Robert Hoskins, *Clara A. Swain, First Medical Missionary to the Women of the Orient* (Boston: W.F.M.S., M. E. Church, 1912); Annie R. Gracey, *op. cit.*, pp. 212-216; Frances J. Baker, *op. cit.*, pp. 118-134; Barclay, *History of Methodist Missions*, II/III, 183; Clara A. Swain, *A Glimpse of India*.

are, excepting in cases of special emergency, well provided for." She related how women would go first to a local uneducated woman healer, then to male practitioners of traditional medicine, next to various sorts of persons pretending to practice "English medicine," all the while receiving no genuine examination beyond taking of the pulse, and finally in great distress going to the missionary doctor. Even then it was likely that the doctor's orders would not be followed. Nevertheless, all such obstacles were overcome again and again, patients came in ever greater numbers, and the reputation of the mission physicians and surgeons rose. Their manifestation of loving concern for their patients as individuals and their mediation of the love of God in Christ for persons were as important as their scientific knowledge and technical skill. The writings and speeches of the women medical missionaries make it clear that they considered themselves evangelists.

Dr. Clara Swain's reputation spread so far afield that in March, 1885, the Rajput Rajah of Khetri asked her to attend his wife. At the end of a two-week visit the ruler requested her to become permanent physician to the Rani. Muslim Khetri was fanatically opposed to Christianity and open evangelism was then impossible. Dr. Swain accepted the appointment primarily for the opportunity of Christian witness. The progressive prince also brought in an Englishwoman to conduct a palace school for girls. The two women worked together. They conducted for their servants a Sunday Bible class and service, which was open also to others. Bible portions and tracts were distributed. A Bible class was held in the Rani's apartments. A dispensary for women was opened. In March, 1895, Miss Swain retired and returned to her home town, although she visited India again for the semicentennial celebration of the Methodist Mission in 1906. Her book, *A Glimpse of India,* was published in 1909.

Dr. Lucilla H. Green, another Philadelphia graduate, took over the Bareilly hospital when Clara Swain went on a sick leave; but two years later she married a missionary, and after moving to Naini Tal succumbed to cholera. Dr. Julia

N. McGrew then directed the work until Dr. Swain's return. When the latter went to Khetri, Dr. Mary F. Christiancy replaced her, and the medical class was resumed. Meanwhile the Methodists had sent their second woman doctor to begin work at Lucknow in 1872, Dr. Nancy Monelle; but after a year she accepted an invitation from the ruler of Hyderabad. Three years later she married a missionary and went with her husband to Moradabad, where she practiced medicine. She was responsible in 1890 for presenting to the Colonial government a petition to raise the legal marriageable age of girls to fourteen years, giving ample medical grounds for such legislation. The age was raised to twelve years, a considerable improvement. Moradabad, Cawnpur, and Baroda became other centers for Methodist women's medical work.

As quickly as they could recruit women physicians, the other American women's foreign missionary societies followed the Methodist example. Presbyterians sent to Allahabad, India, in 1871 Dr. Sara C. Seward, sister of the U. S. minister at Peking and niece of Secretary of State Seward. She died of cholera in service twenty years later. The first Congregationalist woman physician went to Bombay in 1873, Miss Sarah F. Norris. The first of the Baptist lady doctors went to Moulmein, Burma, in 1879 at the age of fifty. She was Eleanor F. Mitchell, who had been an Army nurse in the Civil War and had practiced medicine in Fond du Lac, Wisconsin. With her went a nurse, Miss A. M. Barkley. That same year the Baptists sent Dr. Caroline H. Daniels to Swatow; but others were already serving in China, the first having been the Methodist Dr. Lucinda Coombs, sent to Peking in 1873. Almost each year witnessed the entrance of some woman physician into a new land or region. The English societies began to follow the American example in 1880, when the Church of England Zenana Missionary Society appointed Dr. Fanny J. Butler to India. The death toll of these women appears above average. One at least became a martyr, and her death stimulated the devotion of American women to the cause. She was Eleanor Chestnut, who, left an orphan in infancy, had gained an education by sheer determination.

Graduated at Park College, she took her medical degree at Woman's Medical College in Chicago, followed that with a nursing course, interned at a women's reformatory in Massachusetts, and finally took a course of Bible study at Moody Institute. She went to China first in 1893, and had just returned from furlough to Lienchow in October, 1903, when she and other missionaries there were slain by a mob. Her last act before the death blow was to dress the head wound of a boy in the crowd.[8]

Training national women as physicians was more difficult than curative practice. Christian girls had to be convinced that they could defy tradition and enter the medical profession, but in this the example of the European and American woman was a powerful argument. Resources for teaching were meager. The first medical classes, and even schools, were primitive affairs. By 1900 medical classes were reported to be conducted by American missionaries for or including women at Amoy, Chungking, and Weihsien, China; Seoul, Korea; and Bareilly, India. American medical schools were admitting women at Canton and Soochow, while the Congregationalists had a school solely for women at Foochow. American women were also participating in the North India school of Medicine for Christian Women at Ludhiana. There were training schools or classes in nursing at Inuvil, Ceylon, and at Soochow, China. The Doshisha Nurses Training School at Kyoto, Japan, founded by the American Board in 1887, had been taken over by Japanese administration.

The figures for the next decade, ending in 1910, are puzzling in some respects and require further investigation. Two American medical classes with only three students between them are reported in Korea. Twenty-one United States and Canadian institutions in China were then training sixty-eight men and sixty-nine women. The figures for India appear to show total reliance on Ludhiana for medical instruction, and the American missions were stressing local nursing schools,

---

8 Robert E. Speer, *Servants of the King* (N. Y.: Missionary Education Movement, 1911), pp. 89-113.

of which there were ten. In Persia one lone woman was in training. That is all reported by Dennis, Beach, and Fahs.

However, thirty-seven schools of nursing under American auspices were then operating in Korea, China, Japan, India, the Philippines, Syria, Brazil, Mexico, and Puerto Rico with a total of 199 students. American schools of nursing in South and Southwest Africa at the time had only male students. The statistics indicate that the introduction of the nursing profession was in progress, but still in its initial stages. What appeared to Oriental peoples to be the menial aspects of the service was an obstacle to acceptance. Only loving compassion, caught from God's love of men, could produce vocation until the profession gained prestige. National women doctors soon became visible as proof of the success of the medical ministry, and Dr. Mary Stone of China was to many an incarnation of the whole movement. The nurses were much more obscure, and, of course, even the missionary nurses were not given the recognition nor accorded the fame of the physicians, although their achievement equaled that of the doctors. The 1959 *Directory of Protestant Medical Missions* compiled by the Missionary Research Library reports in service at that date 1,415 missionary nurses and 5,937 national nurses. This indicates both the continuing and growing place nursing assumed in the mission enterprise and the extent to which it had become an accepted profession for women. Were this book not already threatening to exceed its bounds, the writer would search out the "Florence Nightingales" of missionary nursing and commemorate them gratefully. Among them were Miss Elizabeth M. McKechnie (Mrs. Thompson), appointed to Shanghai in 1884 by the Woman's Union Foreign Missionary Society; Miss A. M. Barkley, Burma, 1879; and Miss Ella A. Lewis, Peking, 1891. It appears that no one tabulated the missionary nurses before 1910. That year Mrs. Helen Barrett Montgomery reported that 91 were serving under thirty-six American women's boards, compared with 147 physicians.[9]

---

[9] Helen B. Montgomery, *op. cit.*, end table.

The foregoing paragraphs describe only the beginnings of women's work for women and children under the women's boards. The chief spokesman of those boards at the time of the semicentennial jubilee in 1910, Mrs. Helen B. Montgomery, stated:

> We began in weakness, we stand in power. In 1861 there was a single missionary in the field, Miss Marston, in Burma; in 1909, there were 4710 unmarried women in the field, 1948 of them from the United States. In 1861 there was one organized woman's society in our country; in 1910 there were forty-four. Then the supporters numbered a few hundreds; today there are at least two millions. Then the amount contributed was $2,000; last year four million dollars was raised. The development on the field has been as remarkable as that at home. Beginning with a single teacher, there are at the opening of the Jubilee year 800 teachers, 140 physicians, 380 evangelists, 79 trained nurses, 5783 Bible women and native helpers. Among the 2100 schools there are 260 boarding and high schools. There are 75 hospitals and 78 dispensaries. In addition to carrying on these large tasks, the women's missionary organizations have built colleges, hospitals, dispensaries, nurses' homes, orphanages, leper asylums, homes for missionaries' children, training schools, and industrial plants. They have set up printing presses, translated Bibles, tracts, and school books. They have published missionary magazines, distributed mite boxes, printed millions of lesson leaflets, study outlines, programs, and booklets. They have maintained offices, state and national organizations, yearly and triennial conventions. They have developed a fine network of unpaid helpers with which to cover the entire country. It is an achievement of which women may well be proud.[10]

The program continued to develop along these lines for another fifteen years until integration with the general church boards began to take place, expanding in volume, improving in quality, incorporating some new methods and techniques, and raising up and supporting ever increasing numbers of national women doctors, teachers, nurses, evangelists, and other workers.

---

10 *Ibid.*, pp. 243-244.

Limitation of space forbids adequate attention to the home-base program. Details of organization and denominational variations would be monotonous to the contemporary reader. There was generally a determined effort to establish a local missionary society in every church or charge or to enlist existing societies in the organization. These local societies were then united in a city or county organization or presbyterial, association, or district auxiliary. In some denominations there would be an additional higher level of organization under the national or regional society — the synodical, conference, or state branch. Offices, committees, and programs on all these levels involved thousands of women actively, made them personal participants in the enterprise, and stimulated them to work for the generally accepted goal of making each woman in every local church an active member of a local society. Conventions or assemblies, annual or otherwise, acquainted all these women workers one with another, diffused information, and stimulated zeal.

Most of the boards or societies sought to cultivate the interest of children, teen-age girls, and young women, both to foster a missionary devotion in the churches and to insure a regular flow of new members into the societies. Nearly all societies sponsored Mission Bands, and employed (or delegated to a volunteer worker) a secretary for the department. Primary school-age Bands usually included boys. Although usually called Mission Band, such a group might have the name Busy Bees, Carrier Doves, Lookout Guards, or even Snowflakes. The children elected their own officers, presided over their meetings, participated in programs, heard stories, made maps, acted in dramatizations of missionary anecdotes or pageants, saved pennies in mite boxes, raised money in various other ways, and contributed to some definite project, such as building a chapel, supporting an orphan, or providing a scholarship for a national child in some mission school. The members of the Mission Bands of the Evangelical Church took this pledge:

> I promise each day to pray for the salvation of the heathen.
> I promise to give what money I can to send them the gospel.
> I promise to attend each meeting of our Mission Band if I can.

The first Methodist band was "The Juvenile Missionary Society" formed at Berea, Ohio, in 1873. By 1895 there were 741 Children's Bands under the several branches, the Cincinnati Branch leading with 152. It was much the same in the other denominations. What was reported by the Christian Woman's Board of Missions probably was the experience of others. About 1892 the Christian Endeavor Movement captured many of the bands and contributions to denominational causes decreased, the money being given to local projects. Complaints from denominational officers led the officers of the United Society of Christian Endeavor to counteract this by directing that societies connected with denominational churches should make their contributions to denominational causes through their own societies.

Some of the societies tried "to get them young," meaning really to "get" the young mothers interested. The Methodists made "a place in our missionary fold for the tiny lambs of the flock," and sponsored the Little Light Bearer movement. A baby was to pay, through his mother, twenty-five cents a year for five years. The Women of the Evangelical Church began in 1885 a similar scheme of "Wee Bands," changing the name to Missionary Cradle Roll in 1887. It was expected that on reaching the right age these infants would become members of the Mission Bands.

Societies of teen-age girls and young women were more numerous than the Children's Bands. The Methodists had 810 Young Women's Societies in 1895. The Christian Woman's Board of Missions organized "Circles" which ranked with the adult auxiliaries and contributed to special funds, such as support of schools and native helpers. Originally called Young Women's Missionary Bands in the United Brethren Church, the name was changed to Otterbein Guild of the Woman's Missionary Association. There was a tendency for a particular age-group of girls to stay together and to discourage the entry of younger girls. As they got older, any reason for separation from the adult societies vanished, and eventually in many instances there was amalgamation.[11]

[11 On children and young women: Dwight, Tupper, Bliss, *Ency-*

Accurate information was propagated, interest was stimulated, and zeal was kindled by two principal means, the itineration of missionaries on furlough, and literature. Almost each and every society had its magazine — *Heathen Woman's Friend, Woman's Work for Woman, Woman's Missionary Advocate,* for example — or at least certain columns in the denominational paper. Other magazines, at least for periods, were published for children, such as the American Board-Woman's Board's *Mission Day-Spring,* while some boards, like the Baptists, who gave a page in *The Helping Hand* to "Little Helpers," got some space for children's interests in the adult magazine. Vast quantities of reports, programs, pamphlets, tracts, and historical sketches were printed, and occasionally a book was published. More serious study material was prepared and published cooperatively, as we shall see in the next chapter, and cooperative summer conferences prepared for its use. The editor in each society was an officer of crucial importance to the whole program.

The whole point of organization and promotion was to raise funds to support the overseas program. This meant that on every level — adult, youth, child — there was intensive cultivation of stewardship and systematic giving. There simply had to be this insistence on raising money, *because the special work for women and children was financed by a "second gift,"* the women already having given first to the general budgeted denominational general mission program. The devoted women went a farther distance along the road of self-denial and gave again at real personal cost. Mite boxes were distributed for daily and weekly use, funds were asked for special projects, and especially there was universal reliance on an annual thank offering or love offering. The large sums mentioned in the previous chapter were the result of such systematic giving.

clopedia of Missions, 2nd ed., p. 793; Baker, op. cit., pp. 60-63; Hartford and Bell, History of the Woman's Missionary Association of the United Brethren in Christ, pp. 17-20; Dickinson and Moses, Historical Sketch of the Christian Woman's Board of Missions, Dec. 1907 ed., pp. 63-67; Steinmetz, Reminiscences, pp. 84-90, 105ff.

The whole women's missionary enterprise was undergirded and sustained by intercessory prayer.

There was intimate intercommunication at home and on the fields among the personnel of the various societies and boards, American, British, and European. Consequently there was interaction, and they accommodated largely to a common pattern of program and action. Unity among the American societies in goals, means, and methods is most marked. It was early discovered that some things could best be done in concert and cooperation. To that story we turn in the next chapter.

VI

MISSION IN UNITY

THE WOMEN CREATED THE FIRST INTERNATIONAL ECUMENICAL
missionary agency intended to be universal in scope. William
Carey had proposed a decennial world conference to be held
at the Cape of Good Hope beginning in 1810, but that was
considered one of Carey's wildest and most visionary ideas.
Professor Gustav Warneck at the Centenary Conference,
through a paper read for him, also advocated a worldwide
conference. The boards and societies, however, did not act
along such a line until the World Missionary Conference at
Edinburgh in 1910 established its Continuation Committee.
But twenty-two years earlier the women had dared to establish
an international representative body. Thirty-two leaders of
United States women's foreign boards and four Canadians
participated most vocally in the Centenary Conference in
London, and they induced their British sisters to join them in
creating the World's Missionary Committee of Christian
Women. Miss Abbie B. Child was elected chairman, and upon

her return home she sent an invitation to all women's missionary societies.

This forgotten document of the Ecumenical Movement deserves quotation:

WORLD'S MISSIONARY COMMITTEE OF CHRISTIAN WOMEN

DEAR MADAM:-

At a Woman's Meeting held in connection with the General Missionary Conference in London, June 9 to 19, 1888, it was proposed that a World's Missionary Committee of Christian Women should be established, which should form a means of communication between the different denominational, union and other *great* (not local or parish) societies. The object of such Committee would be to secure concerted action on the part of all Women's, General, Foreign, and Home Missionary Societies: — 1, For special prayer; 2, For united effort for other objects: as, for example, the legal relief of the twenty million of widows in India; 3, For the arrangement of any general conference that may be deemed desirable.

It is suggested that each member of such World's Committee should send annually some communication from her society, either by letter or printed document, to its chairman, and to each society represented thereon.

At the close of this meeting, also, a committee to carry out these suggestions was elected, consisting of the following ladies:-

Miss Abbie B. Child, Chairman, Secretary, Woman's Board of Missions, Congregational House, Boston, Massachusetts, U. S. A.

Mrs. A. S. Quinton, President of the Women's National Indian Association, Philadelphia, Pennsylvania, U. S. A.

Miss Bennett, London Missionary Society.

Miss Mulvany, Secretary of Church of England Zenana Missionary Society, 9 Salisbury Square, Fleet Street, London, E. C.

Miss Reid, Secretary of Scotland Ladies' Association for Foreign Missions, 22 Queen Street, Edinburgh.

Mrs. John Lowe, 56 George Square, Edinburgh.

In addition to these suggestions, this Committee was instructed to invite into its number a representative from each general Woman's Missionary Society desiring to co-operate in the formation of such a World's Committee.

The Committee thus elected earnestly hopes that your Society will join in this movement by electing one of your number to serve thereon, and by notifying the Chairman.

Will you please send word to the undersigned, as soon as possible, whether your Society wishes to be represented in this Committee, and the name and address of the person elected, to

Miss Abbie B. Child
No. 1 Congregational House

Boston, Dec. 29, 1888.   *Boston, Mass., U. S. A.*

There are fifty to sixty letters of positive approval and action in Miss Child's file; and a small notebook lists as members, with the representative of each, nine societies in Great Britain and Ireland, seven in Canada, thirty in the United States, and the lone Woman's Board of Missions for the Pacific far out in the western seas. There are no responses from the Continent of Europe or the British colonies.[1] A weekly intercessory hour of prayer for the world mission appears to have been the first venture sponsored, and the numerous societies were requested to ask their members to pray every Sunday evening between five and six o'clock.

The World's Missionary Committee of Christian Women was in all reality its North American members, although those overseas were involved through correspondence. Only in America was there such a thing as home missions, although similar church extension must have existed then in Australia and New Zealand. The women were far ahead of their time in conceiving of mission as world mission, joining both

---

[1] Division of Overseas Ministries, National Council of Churches of Christ in the U. S. A., "Historical Material: World Day of Prayer and Women's Work," Box 1. This is the only collection of documents relating to the World's Committee, and is the source for this section. It may be noted that the Chicago Conference of 1893 taught the women a costly lesson about the expense of large conferences. They employed a court reporter and stenographer to record the proceedings of the two days and did not have money to pay him! Meeting his bill was a protracted and serious matter.

foreign and domestic aspects of a single task. None of the purely domestic societies joined the Committee, although they participated heartily in the Conference and Congress at Chicago in 1893. The existence and the activities of this World's Missionary Committee of Christian Women reveal the unity and sense of common identity felt by the participants in the women's missionary movement. The American leaders were a closely knit group. They had together founded the Woman's Union Foreign Missionary Society. Forced by denominational pressures then to organize separately, they still kept their sense of solidarity, and conversed, discussed, corresponded, and acted together. The voice and pen of Abbie B. Child were especially powerful instruments in fostering this cohesion.

There were three major achievements of the World's Committee: the conference of women's missionary societies held in connection with the Woman's Congress of Missions as well as assistance in that Congress; the women's work programs, both general and sectional, of the Ecumenical Missionary Conference in New York in 1900; and the Central Committee for the United Systematic Study of Missions.

The Committee members rejected a proposal to meet in Washington in 1891 in favor of a meeting in connection with the Columbian Exposition at Chicago in 1893. When they, under Miss Child's leadership, began to plan for that occasion it was discovered that Chicago women, including members of several Chicago-based women's societies, were planning a Congress of Missions for Women; the World's Committee became auxiliary to it in relation to the Congress set for October 2 to 4, and planned a Conference of Women's Missionary Societies for September 29 and 30. Delegates were apportioned according to the number of local societies in addition to the officers and one delegate from each major society. The Conference dealt with administration and methods of work, leaving inspiration and general information to the Congress. In connection with their meeting, the World's Committee planned for outstanding women experts on missions to tour the land. The famous Isabella Bird Bishop wrote from Lambeth Palace that she was impressed with "the truly American breadth of your projects for me." Only a small contingent of British delegates could attend, headed by the renowned Miss Louisa Whately; but each society sent a report. Distance kept a few Canadian societies from participation, but the others and the general, home, and foreign women's societies of the United States all sent official delegates. Both meetings were a tremendous success and imparted a renewed impetus to the women's missionary movement.

Again it was the American members of the World's Committee who planned the several sessions on women's work in the course of the colossal Ecumenical Missionary Conference, including the unexpected overflow assemblies. They met frequently from 1897 to 1900. Thousands of women came to this conference from across the country, and a few from overseas. It was the most complete and impressive presentation of the world mission ever given the American public. Once more the women received inspiration and had their sense of unity strengthened.

The World's Committee met in connection with the Ecumenical Conference, and its most important action was the creation of the Central Committee on the Systematic Study of Missions. This was expected to be an international project, but it actually served only North American societies. It reported to the Interdenominational Conference of Woman's Boards of Foreign Missions and became increasingly involved with that organization. Consequently it is best treated in connection with that regional organ. Miss Child died suddenly in 1902, and with her passing the World's Committee also passed, although being nominally in existence for a few more years. The Interdenominational Conference was its successor.

It should be noted that sometime before 1900 some of the North American women's societies also had another international relationship. The printed directory of the International Union of Women's Foreign Missionary Societies in Connection with the Reformed and Presbyterian Churches lists eight member societies in Great Britain and Ireland, one in France, one in Switzerland, ten in the United States, two in

Canada, one in South Africa, one in New Zealand, and four in Australia. The president was Mrs. D. A. Cunningham of Wheeling, West Virginia, and the secretary Miss Mathews of the Women's Missionary Association of the Presbyterian Church in England.

The Western Section of the Alliance of Reformed and Presbyterian Churches was responsible for initiating in 1893 the Interdenominational Conference of Foreign Mission Boards of the United States and Canada, later called the Foreign Missions Conference of North America. Women were not invited either as representatives of their societies or as individuals, although for many years there was one lone woman, representing the Philadelphia Friends. Three years later the first Interdenominational Conference of Woman's Boards of Foreign Missions of the United States and Canada was held, comprised of official delegates. The Conference met again in 1898, 1899, 1900, 1901, 1904, 1906, 1909, 1912, 1915, and thereafter annually.

The organization was most informal in early years. The secretary of one year's conference became the chairman of the Committee on Arrangements for the next. The Committee on Arrangements planned the program and appointed a Business Committee to steer the meeting and present resolutions for consideration. It also chose representatives from four boards to be the Committee on Arrangements for the next meeting, the board entertaining the conference adding a fifth member. Programs were printed, but no reports issued until 1904, when a condensed version of the proceedings was "manifolded" for distribution to societies not represented at the meeting. Beginning with 1906 reports were printed. There was little expense except correspondence and the printing of programs, and this was met by a collection taken at one session. There were special sessions held simultaneously one morning or afternoon for secretaries, treasurers, heads of departments such as Young People's Work or Literature, and the World's Missionary Committee. In 1898 and 1901 there was a joint session with the "men's" conference. Papers or lectures on specific topics, such as recruiting and training of missionaries or the ideal missionary magazine, were followed by discussion. All problems of administration, promotion, education, personnel, and methods were brought to the floor. The result was that the larger boards generally approximated a standard pattern and the smaller, newer societies adapted to the model.[2]

A committee charged in 1904 with recommending permanent organization reported in 1906, and a set of by-laws was adopted. Henceforth the president and local corresponding secretary were to be members of the denomination which would entertain the Conference, while continuity and permanence would be provided by the successive reelection of the same secretary. All affairs were left in the hands of the Committees on Arrangements and Business. There was also provision for a Committee on Summer Schools and a Committee on Correspondence with the World's Committee and its member boards. Joint committees of the boards for special work, such as the Committee on United Study of Missions, were to conduct themselves as independent bodies, but render a report regularly and seek to carry out the wishes of the Conference. Meetings were to be triennial. With such a simple structure the Conference got along well and accomplished its design until the great celebration of the semicentennial Jubilee of the women's missionary movement in 1911, which reviewed achievements since the foundation of the Woman's Union Foreign Missionary Society and rallied the women for a forward movement.

The World Missionary Conference at Edinburgh in 1910 had just brought to the multiplicity of sovereign agencies a sense of being engaged together in one single world mission. Its comprehensive surveys had provided a total view of the mission never before so clearly seen by so many. It brought the Western churches into confrontation with the existing young national churches. It gave a tremendous stimulus to

---

2 The sources for the Interdenominational Conference of Woman's Boards of Foreign Missions are its printed Reports from 1906 to 1916 and remaining records in the files of the Federation of Woman's Boards and the Department of Women's Work of the Foreign Missions Conference, in D.O.M., National Council of Churches.

further unity and cooperation in the overseas mission, and from it issued the three strands of the Ecumenical Movement. Its influence among the churches was an invaluable asset to the women in planning and carrying forward their Jubilee celebrations. One hundred sixteen United States and Canadian women participated as official delegates, and hundreds more were there as visitors attending the public meetings. The women had not been given one single place on the Central and American Executive Committees or any other committee, but Mrs. Charles A. Daniels, Miss Grace H. Dodge, and Mrs. William A. Montgomery were members of three of the Preparatory Commissions, and a few others had been among the correspondents. The planning of the Jubilee was as skillful and careful as that of the World Missionary Conference, and the women demonstrated to the men that they were in no way inferior in conceiving and executing grand schemes.

The Jubilee occurred in the midst of a three-year interval between meetings of the Interdenominational Conference, and the planning evidently devolved upon the Central Committee for the United Study of Missions or upon the same women acting as a special committee of the boards, The Jubilee was the idea of Mrs. Henry W. Peabody. She and Mrs. Helen Barrett Montgomery, dynamic officers of the Woman's American Baptist Foreign Mission Society and leaders in the interdenominational fellowship, were the prime movers and organizers. They were the power behind the whole tremendous project. The 1910 United Study program was made a preparation for the celebration. The textbook, Mrs. Montgomery's *Western Women in Eastern Lands,* reviewed the achievements of fifty years and presented the challenge of the present. She also wrote the pageant for the Jubilee. A thank-offering goal of one million dollars was set, to be used largely for the women's Christian colleges in Asia. The mission was brought home dramatically to the women of the nation by forty-eight two-day "great Jubilees" in major cities and by numerous one-day meetings. Local committees of up to four hundred persons prepared for the celebrations. The Jubilees began with Oakland, California, on October 12, 1910, and ran through the winter. They were held at Portland, Seattle, Denver, Omaha, Lincoln, Kansas City, St. Louis, Milwaukee, Minneapolis-St. Paul, Chicago, Indianapolis, Cincinnati, and Detroit before Christmas; and after New Year at Cleveland, Louisville, Nashville, Washington, Richmond, Baltimore, Harrisburg, Philadelphia, Pittsburgh, Buffalo, Atlantic City, Troy, Springfield, New Haven, Providence, Boston, Portland, and Syracuse. One-day meetings filled in the gaps. Everywhere there were to be follow-up campaigns, and the pilot program in Baltimore demonstrated what might be accomplished. Mrs. Peabody reported to the Interdenominational Conference in 1912 that the fruits of the Jubilee were joy, knowledge, faith, prayer, humility, and love expressed in an offering of $1,030,000.[3]

The Jubilee had involved administrative efforts of such magnitude and intensity that the officers of the boards had been convinced that the rudimentary structure of a triennial Conference no longer met their need. Mrs. Peabody brought to the boards, as chairman of the Central Committee on United Study, at a meeting in New York in April, 1911, in connection with the Jubilee in that city, a plan of federation. She presented it again with the comments of the boards at the Ninth Interdenominational Conference in Philadelphia in 1912. The scheme was modified and adopted, and ordered into effect for an experimental period of three years. A report was to be made at the next triennial Conference. This plan sought to combine national and regional features. There were to be four Territorial Commissions in the United States and one in Canada. All societies or boards within the area would make up the Territorial Commission. A Central Commission was formed by two representatives from each Territorial body plus one from the Central Committee for the United Study of Missions.

However, when the matter came again before the Interdenominational Conference in 1915, there was great dissatisfac-

---

[3] Rachel Lowrie, *The Story of the Jubilee; 9th Interdenom. Conf. W.B.F.M.,* 1912, pp. 12-14; file of Jubilee bulletins, programs, etc. in D.O.M. office, National Council of Churches.

tion. It was proposed to merge the Conference and Federation, and make the new organ a federation of the boards and societies themselves directly and not through intermediary regional bodies. The question was assigned to a committee of seven instructed to report the following year. The Conference and Federation then merged at the 1916 meeting. An Executive Committee provided henceforth responsible continuity between annual meetings. There were to be four home-based standing committees: Methods of Work with Women, Young People, and Children; Student Work; Summer Schools and Conferences; Publications and Literature. There were to be two foreign-field standing committees: Christian Literature for Women and Children, and Interdenominational Institutions. Thus the Interdenominational Conference had taken the same path as its counterpart agency had done in becoming the Foreign Missions Conference, but as the result of its own experience, not just to follow the example of the men. The Federation henceforth followed this constitutional pattern until its complete merger with the F.M.C. in 1934.[4]

The major home-base activities of the old Interdenominational Conference were retained and increased under the new order. The first of all the cooperative ventures was the Central Committee for the United Study of Missions, which produced the books and study material for all the women's boards. The origin of this Committee has been related. It had been the inspiration of Abbie B. Child, but she had not lived to see it develop. Its success was primarily due to the leadership of Lucy (Mrs. Henry W.) Peabody of Boston, who became chairman about 1907 and served until 1930, when she became honorary chairman. Mrs. Helen Barrett Montgomery also exerted great influence in this activity. Miss Clementina Butler was secretary in early years. The Committee was formed by one representative each from the Baptist, Congregational, Methodist Episcopal, Presbyterian, and Protestant Epis-

---

4 *9th Interdenom. Conf. W. B. For. Mis., 1921*, pp. 1, 2-3, 4-6; *10th Conf. 1915*, pp. 7-8, 9-10; *11th Conf. 1916;* Federation of Woman's Boards of Foreign Missions, *Annual Report, 1917*, constitution and by-laws on pp. 1-5; Gladys G. Calkins, *Follow These Women*, pp. 12-13.

copal women's foreign boards. Later the Reformed and Lutheran women were also members. This was an independent organization, but, while still retaining its identity, with the establishment of the Federation became the standing committee on Publication and Literature for that body.

Once the Committee had been formed in 1900, it acted with amazing speed, and by autumn had produced for distribution a series of leaflet guides on missions in the nineteenth century and had its first textbook in press. This was *Via Christi,* by Louise M. Hodgkins, a history of missions from the apostles to 1900. Harlan P. Beach of the Student Volunteer Movement told the women, on the basis of experience in the S.V.M., that a history book would never sell and this was a bad choice for initiating study. However, that book sold 50,000 copies! A series of seven annual textbooks was planned and produced, covering India, China, Japan, Africa, the Pacific, and Missions and Social Progress, all written by eminent authorities. Then there followed volumes on the Muslim world; Korea, Burma, and Siam; and Latin America. Before Helen B. Montgomery's Jubilee book on the work with women and children was issued, more than 600,000 copies of these texts had been sold. They and other material were sold to the boards at a discount, and, until the World War cut sales and profits, grants were made out of surplus to other activities of the Interdenominational Conference and Federation. After 1910 the Central Committee became its own publisher, producing both adult and junior textbooks and other supplementary literature. Publications along with a variety of supplies needed by local societies, such as maps and mite boxes, were distributed through a little office in West Medford, Massachusetts, staffed usually by one remarkable woman, Miss Leavis.

The Central Committee published the *Bulletin* of the Federation, and continued to finance it when it was reduced to a section in the *Missionary Review of the World.* It was also the publisher of a magazine for children, *Everyland,* of which Mrs. Peabody was editor and of which she long paid the expense personally.

This Central Committee was in many ways perhaps the

most successful publisher of mission books, but not the only one. The Student Volunteer Movement was the first in the field. Its production of study books was passed over to a new body, the Young People's Missionary Movement, which in turn became the Missionary Education Movement, related to the Foreign Missions Conference. If not a piecemeal approach to missionary educational publishing, there was at least overlap in the approach to the total church membership in the country. There was created in 1914 the Committee of Twenty-Eight to choose annual themes for home and foreign mission study and to bring at least some degree of coordination. It was comprised of seven members each from the Federation of Woman's Boards of Foreign Missions, the Woman's Council of Home Missions (which also had a publication program antedating the Council's formation), the Home Missions Council of North America, and the Foreign Missions Conference.

The ladies of the Central Committee well knew that intensive and widespread study would not spontaneously arise out of publication of textbooks. Local societies must be enlisted in study and above all leaders and teachers must be trained. The great reliance would be placed on summer schools of mission study and training sessions in large centers. The proposal for a summer school was enthusiastically received by the Interdenominational Conference of January 12, 1904, and a committee made responsible for the experiment. That summer the first school was held at Northfield, Massachusetts, from July 12 to 19, and was an immediate success. A battery of excellent teachers taught the course, and there was worship, Bible study, prayer, and consideration of field mission problems along with local home-base cultivation methods. The 235 women enrolled went home on fire with enthusiasm. The Northfield School would be repeated, and next year others were added at Chautauqua, New York, and Winona Lake, Indiana. Such schools rapidly proliferated, and the Council of Women for Home Missions began similar ones for the domestic field. A number arose not clearly affiliated with either body. The new Federation's committee made a determined effort to standardize and upgrade the quality of the schools. The Federation and the Council together established a National School for the training of authorized leaders of summer schools, and it was held for two weeks in the spring, well in advance of the summer schools. In 1917 twenty-five schools had a total of 11,693 women and girls registered. The impact on the churches was tremendous.

Integration of the two systems of schools and the elimination of wasteful overlap were greatly to be desired. Therefore, in 1928 the Federation and the Council merged their separate units in a Joint Committee on Conferences and Schools of Missions. The membership included two women each from the Home and Foreign organizations and the chairmen of all the summer schools affiliated with either of them. By 1930 order was achieved, and although certain schools remained affiliated with only one or the other of the parent agencies, most were jointly sponsored, and separate schools of home and foreign missions were retained only at Northfield and Chautauqua.[5]

Space cannot be given to the other important home-base activities, including most methods for work, special conferences, war work, the peace effort, foreign students, and the like. Student work always got serious attention, and the Student Volunteer Movement and the College Department of the Y.W.C.A. were recognized as recruiting agencies. Contact with college women was effected chiefly through the Y.W.C.A. There was some joint activity in conventions with the Layman's Missionary Movement, which copied the women's movement in some respects. Reports of the Interdenominational Conference and its successor Federation reveal the multiplicity of activities. One important development out of the Jubilee must be mentioned, however, and the development of the World Day of Prayer described.

---

[5] Reports of the Central Committee and of the Committee on Summer Schools appear regularly in the Reports of the Interdenominational Conference W.B.F.M. from 1906-1915, and of the Federation of W.B.F.M. from 1916 through 1933. Annual Reports of the Central Committee were published as leaflets or small pamphlets, and a few have been seen.

Numerous local interdenominational missionary societies or federations arose out of the activity of the Jubilee continuation committees. The women enjoyed the freedom and fellowship of such grass roots ecumenicity. The Federation saw in these local bodies a means of involving the women in the totality of mission and in world affairs beyond what could be done solely through denominational societies. Further organization was stimulated, and for a short period an able woman was engaged to cultivate the field. The movement grew spontaneously even through the war years, and a Federal Council of Churches canvass in 1924 found 1,200 such local interdenominational groups. The Federation in 1918 received from the Council of Women for Home Missions a request for the formation of a joint committee aimed at creating new local federations, councils, or committees; bringing into affiliation with the national bodies such as already existed; promoting unified mission and Bible study for them; and sponsoring a single annual day of united prayer. The response was favorable, and the Joint Committee was created. It became known as the Committee on Women's Church and Missionary Federations.

Over the years there was much discussion with the Federal Council of Churches on local interdenominational women's councils. Conferences were held, such as the St. Louis Conference on Women's Organized Interdenominational Work, May 31 — June 1, 1927. This conference was one of the progressive steps in the search for a solution of the problem of the local interchurch movement, initiated in 1924, when the Federal Council invited the two women's mission agencies into consultation on the matter. The St. Louis Conference voiced the need of an interdenominational national organization through which local work might be correlated, systematized, and promoted. The next year, at a conference in Buffalo on May 30, the National Commission of Protestant Church Women was organized, with Mrs. John Ferguson as chairman and Mrs. Josephine M. Stearns as executive secretary. The Federation gave approval for a trial period of three years. Meantime things were moving too slowly for a number of local leaders and their constituency who could not understand the slowness and caution of official bodies. They brought matters to a conclusion by organizing in June, 1929, the National Council of Federated Church Women, and then proposing merger with the Commission. No other course was now possible, and the Commission capitulated. The National Council of Federated Church Women took its place as an independent ecumenical agency alongside the Federation of Woman's Boards of Foreign Mission, the Council of Women for Home Missions, the Federal Council of Churches, and other agencies. A tripartite Committee on relationships worked out the allocation of responsibilities among the three national women's organizations. Since all had special interest in the World Day of Prayer, International Relations, and Conferences and Schools of Missions, there were to be joint committees for those concerns.[6]

The World Day of Prayer is one of the most remarkable home-base developments, and it evolved into a universal institution. Its origins are obscure, for it springs from the centuries-old practice of intercessory prayer in the overseas mission, from the Monthly Concert of Prayer for Missions which evolved gradually from 1744 to 1796 and well into the nineteenth century,[7] and from many schemes of intercession in the several missionary societies and boards. The women eventually wanted a definite date to commemorate as the beginning, and they seized upon 1887. It was in that year that Mrs. Darwin R. James, president of the Woman's Board of Home Missions of the Presbyterian Church in the U. S. A., induced her Board to set a Week of Humiliation and Prayer ending with the last Sunday in February, one day of which was to be observed with a service of confession of national and individual sins and with an offering fitting to show contrition. Some Methodist, Congregational, Episcopal, Baptist, and Reformed local

---

6 Federation of Woman's Boards of Foreign Missions, *Annual Report, 1916-1933;* Mrs. Fred S. Bennett, *et al., The Emergence of Interdenominational Organization among Protestant Church Women;* Calkins, *op. cit.,* pp. 13-32.

7 R. Pierce Beaver, "The Concert of Prayer for Missions," *Ecumenical Review,* X, 4 (July 1958), 420-427.

societies later accepted the practice. This may be taken as the origin of the Home Mission Day of Prayer, one of the two traditions later to be joined.

The tradition behind the foreign mission Day of Prayer, held on a Friday in January, is difficult to trace. A day of intercession for missions was introduced into the Church of England in 1872 at the suggestion of the Society for the Propagation of the Gospel in Foreign Parts and with the concurrence of the Church Missionary Society. Other British societies may have adopted the practice, because the present writer has somewhere seen a letter, probably from the Interdenominational Conference of Foreign Missionary Societies of the U. S. and Canada, asking the American mission boards to observe the same day as their British brethren — January 10 that particular year. There was a tradition among the women that the original call to prayer came from India about 1860 for the keeping of Thursday in the January week of prayer. One of the earliest actions of Miss Abbie B. Child as chairman of the World's Missionary Committee was to request the member societies to observe the hour from five to six o'clock each Sunday as a time of prayer for the progress of the kingdom of God. Most North American societies responded warmly, while the British members approved the practice, but left the time to individuals, since many women were at that particular hour engaged in Sunday school work. The correspondent for the Cumberland Presbyterian Woman's Foreign Missionary Society informed Miss Child that the Society and its missionaries had kept that practice at that very time since the founding of the organization in 1880. The general Interdenominational Conference of foreign boards issued frequent calls to prayer and sometimes sent them to its feminine counterpart. Thus in 1909 there was such a request to set apart the week of February 21-28 in prayer for the Muslim world.[8]

The first general discussion of the subject took place in the

_____

[8] Miss Abbie B. Child's files in the D.O.M. office, N.C.C.C.U.S.A.; *Interdenom. Conf. W.B.F.M., 1909,* p. 4.

women's Conference at the 1912 annual meeting. At least five boards were then observing a day or week of prayer, most of them in January. It was "voted that the Conference recommend to the Woman's Boards the observance of an interdenominational Day of Prayer during the first week of January on the day appointed for prayer for foreign missions." Facing demobilization and reordering of national life after the War, the Federation of Woman's Boards at its meeting of January 13, 1919, adopted a resolution to join with the Council of Women for Home Missions to "call the women of America to observe twelve o'clock noon of each day as a time of prayer to Almighty God." Perhaps it was this joint action which led the two national women's organizations that very year to combine their separate observances and promote a united Day of Prayer.

This is the immediate origin of the World Day of Prayer. The Executive Committee appointed a committee to join with a like group from the Council to prepare a call and a program for a joint Day of Prayer on February 20. The domestic mission day was thus adopted. The first Friday in Lent would henceforth be the time. The theme was "The Soul of Democracy — Christian Service." Promotion cards and programs were distributed through the Central Committee office in West Medford. The observance apparently made no great impression that first year and there was no mention of it in the 1920 meeting, nor in 1921, but the Treasurer's report contains a few items relative to expenditures. Mrs. Worrell states that the theme for 1920 was "Christ for the World We Bring," that 150,000 calls were sent out and 70,000 programs printed, and that an offering of seventy dollars was sent to the Joint Committee. By January, 1922, it could be reported to the Federation that the Joint Committee had worked out a procedure so as to care for all expenditures, and that an effort was being made to bring the Canadian Boards into the observance. After three years the Day of Prayer had become an established "tradition."

The annual Minutes of the Federation from 1923 onward include a report of the Committee on the World Day of Prayer, and these annual accounts reveal the steady progress in participation and the fostering of unity. Moreover, within five years the institution actually became worldwide, as American missionaries carried the practice to the lands in which they served. The 1926 report first mentions the offering, stating that in 1925 it had amounted to $3,623.66, of which the Council received $1,823.23 for migrant work, and the Federation $1,800.42 for women's colleges in Asia and for literature for women and children. An innovation of 1926 was the provision of a program for a retreat for leaders prepared by Mrs. Charles K. Roys and a sheet of suggestions for program. A questionnaire was sent out broadcast in a restudy of aims and plans. The title "World Day of Prayer" was fixed in 1927. Prepared and printed programs increased the sense of unity as all used the same material.

The chairman of the Committee informed the Federation in 1928: "It has been thrilling to read the many unsolicited letters which have come from India, China, Korea, Japan, South America, Africa, Syria, Europe, the Islands, Canada, and all parts of the United States, telling of the helpfulness of the day, and expressing great joy that it has been made world inclusive." Because of the increasing international character of the observance, the women members of the International Missionary Council's Committee were made advisory members of the Joint Committee, and by 1930 women in forty countries were participating. The program of that year was of international authorship — by the Misses Helen Kim of Korea, Esperanza Abellera of the Philippines, and Jean Paxton of the United States. The offering of that year amounted to $20,000, and the cost of material was more than covered by sales. The question of international administration was now seriously raised, but the more pressing problem was on the American front because the National Council of Federated Church Women had come into being.

The story of what then happened belongs to the next chapter on "Integration."[9]

This has been a most sketchy review of the development of the multiplicity of home-base programs and activities. They were all directed to helping the Woman's Boards of Foreign Missions enlist the women and girls of the churches in the world mission, to educate them to responsibility in national and international affairs, and to gain their support for certain phases of the overseas mission work which the Boards could not do well individually but could do cooperatively, namely the sponsorship of women's colleges and the preparation of literature for women and children.

Intelligent women could scarcely be concerned about effective literature production in the homeland and not be attentive to the even more basic supply of effective literature in the mission fields. It is not surprising that the initial proposal came from the chairman of the Central Committee for the United Study of Missions, Mrs. Peabody. She raised the question at the 1909 Conference, saying to the members: "I feel very keenly the importance of a united movement to give the women of the Orient a helpful literature, not only on Christian themes, but on hygiene, care of children, and the like." The Conference, after discussion, voted a committee to investigate and report. Therefore, at the next meeting in 1912 Miss Clementina Butler read a paper as the report of that special committee. She told her hearers: "New conditions among the nations demand expansion of our activities. The women of the Orient, whom we have taught to read, will desire more than one line of information. In this new day for the womanhood of the far East, we must use the story, the historical incident, the illustration from every day life, to inculcate the truth we desire to present." Agnostic literature was flooding Japan and other lands, she reported. The Bible Societies and the great general boards were providing Bibles and books for intelligentsia. It is the role of the women's

---

[9] *Interdenom. Conf., 1912*, pp. 4, 25; Federation of W.B.F.M., *Annual Report, 1920*, p. 13; *1921; 1922*, pp. 23-26; *1922*, pp. 16, 26; Ruth M. Worrell, *The Day Thou Gavest, The Story of the World Day of Prayer*, p. 7.

boards together to "send in humbler ways the water of life into the very hearts and homes of women and children." Something was being done in India and elsewhere, but not enough. China and the Muslim world were urgently needing literature. Periodicals appeared to be the first need.

The committee put two proposals before the Conference: first, the formation of a Commission in the United States, which would canvass the fields for existing literature, prepare lists of desirable material, secure patronesses for the movement, seek endowment for periodical literature in each field, secure the appointment of at least one woman expert in each field, and publicize the movement; second, the formation of a Commission in each large field, which would collate information on existing material and that in preparation, request the views of each mission on needed literature, communicate such information to the U. S. A. Commission twice a year, estimate costs, advise on publication, promote a magazine for women or for children in each major vernacular language, secure the best translators and illustrators, and place such literature in schools and libraries. The report was accepted, the Commission established, and the members were to be those nominated by the Woman's Baptist Foreign Mission Society (Boston), Woman's Board of Missions, Congregational (Boston), Woman's Foreign Missionary Society of the Methodist Episcopal Church, "the New York Presbyterian Board," and the National Board of the Young Women's Christian Associations.

The name of the new organization was called at first the Interdenominational Committee on Christian Literature for Oriental Women. It added to its membership representatives of the Episcopal Auxiliary and the Woman's Board of the Reformed Church, and it organized with Miss Alice M. Kyle as chairman and Miss Gertrude E. MacArthur of the Y.W.C.A. as secretary. Mrs. Peabody was made a member *ex officio.* The first project immediately undertaken was a children's monthly, the *Chinese Everyland,* with the aid of a Canadian Presbyterian missionary in Shanghai, Mrs. Donald MacGillivray.[10] It was soon renamed *Happy Childhood*. Since China was selected for the first country of emphasis, grants were also made to establish the *Women's Messenger*. Support of these two magazines was continued until after 1950 when the new Communist government cut off all foreign subsidy to Christian work.

The Committee was eventually incorporated in 1934 under the name Committee on Christian Literature for Women and Children in Mission Fields. It profited greatly by continuity in leadership. Only three women served as chairmen until long after the integration of the Federation with the Foreign Missions Conference: Miss Alice Kyle, 1912-1928, Mrs. Helen B. Montgomery, 1928-1930, and Miss Clementina Butler, 1930-1945. Miss Butler was an early secretary, and Miss Olivia Lawrence served in that capacity from 1918 until 1934. Miss Lila V. North was treasurer from 1912 to 1919, and Miss Kyle from 1919 to 1930. The Women's Boards contributed to the expenses, and contributions from local sources were cultivated. Beginning in 1925 the World Day of Prayer offerings made contributions, and eventually this became the most substantial source of support of the annual budget. Mrs. Peabody left the Committee a small bequest, and in 1955 a large one came from Mrs. George W. Doane. Magazines continued to be stressed. A weekly called *Light of Love* for coolie women in Japan was subsidized from 1919 to 1950. *The Treasure Chest* was begun in India in 1922, *Gente Nueva* for youth in Chile in 1928, a Korean magazine for children in 1929, and Africa finally came into the picture in 1930 with *Listen*. Other magazines followed in later years, and other literature was produced with the Committee's aid, such as picture books for children and an African Home Library of more than one hundred little booklets. Since the story has been told by Miss

---

10 *Interdenominational Conference of W.B.F.M., 1909*, pp. 6, 18; *1912*, pp. 3, 21-23; *1915*, pp. 8, 16-19.

Sue Weddell in *More Than Paper and Ink,* covering the first fifty years, the reader is referred to that source for details.[11]

The other great cooperative venture was the stimulation of the foundation of women's colleges and the creation of union boards for them on the field and in North America — for administration in the one instance and for the promotion of financial support in the other. Discussion at the 1906 Conference led to a consensus that it was not wise to bring young women from Asia to the United States for education. However, the corollary, that higher education for them should be provided in Asian lands, was not voiced until the 1915 triennial meeting. By that time pressure in the form of numerous graduates of the high-grade high schools was becoming intense in some quarters. Some portion of the great Jubilee offering of 1911 had been put into buildings and endowment for such colleges, it was said.

Once again Mrs. Peabody and Mrs. Montgomery provided the impetus for a new union venture. They had been active in the Commission on Education of the Edinburgh Conference Continuation Committee and the two of them had just made a journey through the Orient. Each addressed the Conference of 1915 on observations made on the trip, and Mrs. Montgomery read a paper on the higher education of women. Moreover, the president-elect of the new union Christian Women's College of Madras, Miss Eleanor McDougall of Scotland, made an address. Mrs. Montgomery reported, seconded by the others, that Isabella Thoburn College was the only women's college in India at the time, and that Christian girls were entering the "men's colleges" in considerable numbers at some risk of danger. In Madras Presidency alone one hundred Christian girls were engaged in college education. Ginling College had just been established by the joint action of several American missions in Nanking, China. The situation was urgent in Tokyo. The opportunity to lead in women's higher education was open, and "it should be the crown of our whole system."

---

11 Sue Weddell, *More Than Paper and Ink;* Interdenom. Conf. W.B.F.M., *Reports, 1909-1915;* Federation of W.B.F.M., *Annual Reports, 1916-1933.*

It was then and there decided that there must be in the United States a union agency for the conduct of such schools, the holding of property, and the promotion of their support. It was voted to create a committee comprising representatives of the nine American boards cooperating in Ginling and Madras Colleges, to confer with the Commission on Education of the Edinburgh Continuation Committee and, if the outcome were favorable, to prepare a plan for submission to the boards. Organization of the cooperative body was to be effected when a majority of the nine boards concurred in the proposal. Actually incorporated committees or boards for separate institutions were sought, and from its establishment in 1916 onward the Federation of Woman's Boards of Foreign Missions promoted that whole enterprise through its Committee on Interdenominational Institutions on the Foreign Field.

Woman's Christian College, Madras, and Ginling College set the pattern. Six British and seven North American societies cooperated in Madras: Church Missionary Society, Church of England Zenana Missionary Society, Church of Scotland Women's Association for Foreign Missions, London Missionary Society, United Free Church of Scotland Women's Foreign Mission, Wesleyan Methodist Missionary Society's Women's Auxiliary, Woman's American Baptist F.M.S., Woman's F.M.S. of the Methodist Episcopal Church, the Woman's Board of Foreign Missions of the Reformed Church in America, the W.F.M.S. of the Presbyterian Church in Canada, and Woman's Home and Foreign M.S. of the Evangelical Lutheran Church. Administration on the field was under the College Council, composed of two members from each cooperating mission. The principal and faculty composed the Senate for directing internal affairs. There was a Board of Governors, composed of two members from each society, one-half in Britain and one-half in North America. Each member society contributed at least $1,000 annually. Ginling was a union enterprise of the Woman's American Baptist, Christian Woman's, Methodist Episcopal W.F.M.S., Southern Methodist Woman's Missionary Council, and Presbyterian U. S. A. general denominational boards. Each contributed $10,000 for college plant and

$1,500 annually. A representative Board of Control in China administered the school, and the related board in America was the Ginling College Committee of the Trustees of the University of Nanking.

By 1917 six denominations were moving ahead with plans to establish the Union Woman's Medical College at Vellore, India, and five in Woman's Christian College of Japan at Tokyo. Moreover, the Committee was promoting interest in union institutions for which there was no North American board of control: West China Union Normal School for Young Women at Chengtu (1915), Bible Teachers' Training School for Young Women at Nanking (1912), the North China Union Woman's College at Peking (1908), the Woman's Union Medical College of Peking (1910), and the Union Bible Training School at Peking (1915). When the Presbyterians joined the Methodists in the maintenance of Isabella Thoburn College in 1917, that school also was included in the annual reporting. The North China Union Woman's College became the Women's College of Yenching University. An effort was made to interest the Association of College Women in the overseas schools. Wellesley adopted Women's College of Yenching as a sister institution, and Smith College did the same with Ginling.[12] The development of the union colleges had the effect of stimulating and upgrading numerous other denominational colleges.

The year 1919/20 brought notable developments. Seeking greater integration and more effective service, the several college boards in the country united in the Union Committee on Interdenominational Colleges for Women. The Federation of Women's Boards sent a deputation to the East under the general chairmanship of Mrs. Peabody, comprising seven commissions, including one on collegiate education. Chairman of this commission's Japan and China section was President

---

[12] See reports of the Interdenom. Conf. and of the Federation of W.B.F.M. through 1930, for reports of the Committee on Interdenominational Institutions.

Ellen F. Pendleton of Wellesley, and of the India-Egypt section, President Carey Thomas of Bryn Mawr. Three mission board secretaries and various experts were included. The medical commission, headed by Dr. Gertrude H. Walker, studied medical education for women as well as other parts of the medical mission work. The deputation reports were informative and stimulating, and that on collegiate education along with the one on medical education produced immediate action.

An interchurch budget of $6,000,000 was recommended as follows: Madras $300,000, Vellore $500,000, Isabella Thoburn $200,000, Yenching Women's College $1,000,000, Peking Women's Medical College $1,000,000, Ginling $832,000, Tokyo $950,000, and a new women's union medical college in Shanghai to be built upon the relocated Soochow school $1,000,000. However, this ambitious goal was part of the Inter-Church World Movement campaign, which failed. Thereupon the Federation's Committee set out to raise an "International Christmas Gift" of $1,000,000 in 1921 to be gathered in 100,000 gifts of ten dollars each, and Miss Hilda Olson was employed to visit college campuses and present the need. The Christmas Gift brought in $217,000, but boards and friends gave $300,000, and the Laura Spelman Rockefeller Fund gave $250,000. The Joint Committee then decided that the seven union colleges and medical schools needed $3,000,000 more for land and equipment, and the Laura Spelman Rockefeller Memorial Fund promised to give one-third the sum if the remainder were secured by January 1, 1923. Mrs. Peabody became chairman of the campaign. The Federation's Student Committee with the cooperation of the Y.W.C.A. worked the campuses, and the interest of the American Association of University Women was secured. Sixteen mission boards cooperated. When the deadline arrived the fund was short of the goal by about $93,000 cash, but there were outstanding pledges of $112,000. The final accounting showed gifts of $2,854,618 (including the Rockefeller grant) and other

income, bringing the total to $2,942,555. The Federation gave
Mrs. Peabody a rising vote of thanks.[13]

The Joint Committee of the Women's Union Christian
Colleges had twelve able women and three influential men —
James L. Barton, W. I. Chamberlain, and Robert E. Speer —
as members. The name was changed in 1924 to Cooperating
Committee for Women's Union Christian Colleges in Foreign
Fields, supposedly indicating closer and more intensive collab-
oration. Mrs. Montgomery was chairman, and Miss Florence
Tyler executive secretary. Contributions began to come from
"sister colleges," summer conferences, individuals, and World
Day of Prayer offerings. The sum of $955.71 received in the
first year seems woefully small, but was a token of things to
come. Actual administrative work was done by this committee, while the Federation's Committee on Interdenominational Institutions publicized the schools, recommended
those to receive World Day of Prayer money, and generally
stimulated support. As World Day of Prayer offerings grew in
magnitude, they became the principal source of the annual
grants remitted to the colleges apart from the gifts of the
member mission boards controlling each of them.

Ginling and Vellore may be taken as examples of what this
all meant in terms of actual institutional development, and
Mrs. Thurston and Dr. Ida Scudder as representative of the
women who invested their lives in such enterprises.

By the time of the Revolution of 1911 missionaries had
been operating high schools for girls in China for about
seventy years and the government had made some provision
only four years earlier, in 1907. Chinese popular opinion was
still cold to higher education for women; but some of the
graduates of those schools were demanding it, and the church
needed more highly educated women for its service. Two
high schools in Nanking and Canton then offered one or two
years of advanced study, and in Peking the North China

---

13 Federation of W.B.F.M., *Annual Reports, 1919-1924;* file of Cooperating Committee of Women's Union Christian Colleges in D.O.M. office,
National Council of Churches.

Union College for Women, organized in 1908, was just coming into being. A few young women went to the United States for college education. The Revolution was hailed by progressives as ushering China into modernity, and great stimulus was given the desire for Western learning and a mastery of English. Christian schools suddenly found themselves extremely popular. The fifteen mission high schools for girls in the Yangtze valley were put under pressure to provide for their graduates who wanted college education.

The women missionaries of the region were wise and practical enough to discern that no one mission could provide a college of high enough quality and that there must be a union school. Women simultaneously representing eight high schools and eight missions conferred together in Shanghai during the winter of 1911/12. They presented a joint appeal to the women's societies in the United States. Five boards responded positively — American Baptist, Disciples, the Methodists North and South, and Presbyterian U. S. A. Each board pledged $10,000 in capital funds, suport of a teacher, and an annual grant of not less than $600 — a meager commitment on which to build a first-rate college! Each mission appointed three representatives to the Board of Control in China. The college was for legal purposes put under the Board of Trustees of the University of Nanking and awarded degrees under its charter, administration being the responsibility of a Ginling College Committee composed of board representatives. The college was separately incorporated in 1935 with its own Trustees and empowered to grant its own degrees.

The Woman's Board of Foreign Missions of the Presbyterian Church appointed a Congregationalist to the faculty of the new college, and she was elected President. She was Matilda Smyrell Calder Thurston (1875-1958), a graduate of Mt. Holyoke College, who had taught for four years in the Middletown (Connecticut) High School and two years at Marash College in Turkey, then had married J. Lawrence Thurston and gone with him to China in 1902 to found the Yale University Mission at Changsha. Almost at once her husband was invalided home with tuberculosis, and died in

1904. Mrs. Thurston spent two years as traveling secretary of the Student Volunteer Movement, and then from 1906 to 1911 taught in the Yale High School and worked in the hospital under the mission in Changsha. She had, therefore, a thorough acquaintance with China and the problems of education in the land when she returned under the new appointment in 1913. She proved an effective leader of the team of Chinese and missionary teachers and led them in the creation of one of the most highly esteemed colleges in the country. She piloted Ginling College through its organization, establishment, expansion, the difficulties of the turbulent times, and stepped aside under nationalist pressures in 1928 to make way for a Chinese president, Dr. Wu Yi-Fang. But she remained at Nanking as President Emeritus until 1943, except for an interval of three years, teaching, supervising building construction, and aiding her successor. After the Japanese occupation of Nanking and the experience of internment, Mrs. Thurston was repatriated through a civilian exchange; she died at Auburndale, Massachusetts, on April 19, 1958, at the age of eighty-two.[14]

The college, housed in an old mansion, opened its doors in September, 1915; and out of the thirteen students who entered that year, five graduated in 1919, the first women to earn the A.B. degree in China. The spirit and forms of Chinese architecture were employed in the design and construction of a new building occupied in 1923. English and Music were given special stress in the first years because of the demand for them, and Education was soon made a third specialty because of the need of teachers in the Christian schools and throughout the land. Then the demand for teachers in the sciences, social sciences, and physical education led to additional stress on those subjects. A good general arts and sciences curriculum embraced them all in balance. Nearly 60 percent of the graduates became teachers. About 26 percent eventually mar-

---

[14] Presbyterian Church in the U. S. A., Board of Foreign Missions, "Memorial Minute, Matilda Calder Thurston, 1875-1958," adopted at Board Meeting, April 23, 1958, mimeographed; obituary notices, *New York Times* and *New York Herald Tribune,* April 20, 1958.

ried, indicating that higher education had opened to women
other alternatives. Apart from the teaching of the Chinese
classics instruction was in English, because a large part of the
student body came from the dialect-speaking areas of the
country, and shared a written language but not a spoken one.
This student body exceeded 250 by the mid-1930s. The faculty
was never as large as desired, but adequate for an institution of
that size. The students came largely from the wealthy gentry
and from modest Christian families. Christians formed about
two-thirds of the students, and Christian witness was strong.
Many became Christians during their student years. Ginling
had to register with the government in 1930 and meet the
Ministry of Education's requirements in control by Chinese,
an administration headed by a Chinese president, a rigidly
prescribed curriculum, and inspection. Mandatory instruction
in religion was excluded, but the college kept its Christian
character.

The achievements of the college and its faculty seem
incredible when viewed against the confusion and turmoil
of the years of its existence. The college began its career just
when nationalism first seized the students of China. The
Student Patriotic Movement involved the girls in demonstra-
tions and strikes, but also firmly enlisted them in nation
building. Nanking was the battlefield of warlord armies in
1924-1925. The next two years were a period of student anti-
Japanese and antiforeign agitation. In 1927 Nanking was
again the focus of civil war, when the Southern armies sweeping northward in unification of the country captured the city
in March. Occupation of the city took an antiforeign turn,
and there was much looting and some killing. The American
faculty members were removed to Shanghai, but returned
for the opening of the new academic year in the autumn
against the wishes of the Department of State. Japanese
military incursions into China disrupted in 1932. Then after
a few years of peace and progress in the mid-1930s favorable
to educational development, the Japanese invasion began in
earnest in 1937. Centers for Ginling students were established
in cooperation with other Christian colleges in Shanghai,

Wuchang, and Chengtu, and the faculty dispersed among them. Eventually Ginling was removed to Chengtu beyond the battle lines in the west until the end of the war, contending with air raids, lack of facilities, and the difficulties involved in overcrowding in that refugee center.

An emergency committee under Miss Minnie Vautrin remained on the campus in Nanking. During the capture and rape of the city and the period of terror that long followed December 13, more than 10,000 refugees were crowded into the campus. Miss Vautrin fed and protected them, set up schools, established Bible classes, taught them crafts so that they might partially support themselves, and interceded with the Japanese officials for the reunion of families. When war came between the Japanese and the United States, the remaining missionaries were interned in Shanghai, and the campus was taken over for military purposes. When the war ended in August, 1945, it was in sad plight, and rehabilitation proceeded slowly. The college reopened in September, 1946. Recovery was cut short by the advent of the Communist regime. During the first year and a half after the Communist take-over the college was able to continue by making adjustments, but in 1950 the government merged Ginling and the University of Nanking with other schools into the National Ginling University. Subsequent reorganization destroyed the last vestiges of the college and the property was expropriated. But more than a thousand graduates of Ginling were dispersed through the country and abroad, and it could confidently be hoped that the spirit and the lasting contribution of the college would strengthen their Christian faith and enable them to keep their integrity in the new situation.[15]

Vellore is synonymous with Dr. Ida Sophia Scudder, and is today the pride and glory of medical missions. It is the prime exhibit of cooperation and mission in unity. Fifty missions out of ten nations join in supporting the medical college and its hospital. The story of Dr. Ida and Vellore cannot be told in a

---

[15] Matilda S. (Mrs. Lawrence) Thurston, and Ruth M. Chester, *Ginling College* (N. Y.: United Board for Christian Colleges in China, 1955).

page or two and readers are referred to books that deal more adequately with them. Ida Scudder was born at Ranipet in the Arcot District of South India on December 9, 1870, daughter of a medical missionary of the Reformed Church and granddaughter of the very first American medical missionary. Ida was educated at Northfield Seminary, and immediately after graduation went back to India as a short-term missionary because of her mother's illness. A dramatic experience turned the young woman to her medical vocation. In the course of one night a Brahmin, a Muslim, and another high-caste Hindu came to the Scudder residence and each begged the young woman to aid his young wife, then in difficult childbirth. She offered to assist her father, but each husband said that no man could attend his wife. That night all three wives died. Ida then and there dedicated her life to the health and welfare of the women of India. She returned to the United States to study medicine at the Women's Medical College of Philadelphia and completed her course at the Cornell University Medical School in New York. On January 1, 1900, she landed in India with a gift of $10,000 for the erection of a women's hospital in Vellore.

Out of the new hospital there soon developed a branch at Gudiyatham and a series of roadside clinics, extensive treatment of leprosy through the countryside, and a tuberculosis sanitorium at Punganur. In-patients numbered in the thousands and out-patients in the tens of thousands. A few American doctors and nurses could not meet the need of the women and children of South India. So Dr. Ida set out to form a medical college for women. It required five years of continuous persuasion, until in 1918 the Surgeon General gave permission provided that an entering class of five students could be secured. Eighteen entered, and fourteen graduated, all of them successfully passing the government examinations. Five other missions joined the Reformed Church in maintenance of the college, and the united campaign for $3,000,000 for union women's colleges mentioned above brought the funds needed to erect the buildings. Dr. Scudder returned to America and participated enthusiastically in the campaign, and also raised large sums for the new associated hospital and for special requirements of the program. Soon Vellore graduates were making a tremendous impact on the health situation of women and children in South India. Dr. Ida's contagious spirit was caught by them.

Dr. Scudder's long career was crowned by the installation of her distinguished pupil, Dr. Hilda Lazarus, as her successor as principal and director of the college and hospital, and by a radical transformation of the status of the college. When the Christian Medical Association of India determined that there must be established a national, internationally-inter-denominationally supported, coeducational medical school of highest quality, there was no question that it ought to be erected on the already excellent foundation of Vellore. It was no light thing, however, for Dr. Scudder and those who had faithfully supported her to turn from complete devotion to women and children to such an inclusive object. The outcome was assured when Dr. Scudder gave approval and support, for the governing and supporting bodies accepted her judgment, even though a few old friends of the work were lost. Quickly, more than forty missions (now increased to fifty-six) rallied to the cause. All requirements of increased staff, the number of hospital beds, equipment, and the like were met. The first class studying for the M.B., M.S. degree entered in 1942. Men students came in 1947 and were heartily welcomed, but continuity in the training of women was guaranteed. Provisional affiliation with Madras University was changed to permanent status in 1950, and announced at the great jubilee celebration of Dr. Ida's fifty years of medical ministry at Vellore. She died at her home at Kodaikanal May 24, 1960.[16]

---

[16] Mary P. Jeffery, *Ida S. Scudder of Vellore*, jubilee edition (Mysore: Wesley Press, [1951]), and bound with it *Ida S. Scudder and Her Gleam*, memorial supplement, 1961; Dorothy C. Wilson, *Dr. Ida* (N. Y.: McGraw-Hill, 1959). For an estimate of the quality and influence of Vellore, see Edward M. Dodd, *The Gift of the Healer* (N. Y.: Friendship, 1964), pp. 166-168; and for the range of medical services see *Directory of*

This great teaching-healing institution educates doctors, men and women, nurses, medical technicians, and pharmacists. It offers almost every kind of special medical service. It has a public health program. Patients come to it from all over India. On every hand one hears that this is the best medical center in India. Added to scientific and technical skill people find there warmth, kindness, love, the living spirit of the Great Physician.

Protestant Church-Related Hospitals (N.Y.: Missionary Research Library, 1963), p. 81, entry no. 867.

VII

INTEGRATION AND SEQUEL

THE WOMEN'S FOREIGN MISSIONARY SOCIETIES WERE THE MEANS through which American churchwomen achieved involvement and full participation in world mission. They proved conclusively the validity of the causes for which women contended in the formation of those organizations — adequate work for women and children and full opportunity in missionary service for single women. They also educated and marshalled the lay forces of the church in support of overseas missions to an extent never achieved by the denominational boards in the preceding period. Those general boards came to the recognition of the importance of work for women and children and to the effectiveness of the ministry of single women. From the women's boards they also learned the importance of education and promotion, to which they had previously given scant attention. But it was only in their own societies that the women were able to get a role in policy-making, determination of strategy, and administration. It was the power of the women's movement that won for wives as well as unmarried women full status as "missionary" and an equal vote with men in the field missions. Had the men who controlled the general church boards given women a real share in home-base activities and field ministry, the women would not have organized their own boards.

Eventually the two types of boards came to a *modus vivendi* in cooperation. Some male secretaries and directors appreciated female accomplishments and welcomed participation by the women's boards, but there were far more who were never reconciled to the fact of their existence. There were repeated efforts made to subordinate them, and, if possible, to absorb them.

The first decade of the twentieth century was a time of increasing agitation for the integration of the women's societies into the general foreign mission boards. It was frequently alleged that the women were competing as rivals with the official church organizations. Money was supposedly deflected from the denominational budget. Pastors and higher central officials disliked their inability to control such funds, and this second line of giving went against the trend toward centralization. Many thought the church lost what the women gained. There was talk about confusion and duplication in administration, promotion, and finance on both the home and foreign fields. Male administrators and missionaries often said that the women threw the program out of balance, since too much money and personnel were put into work for women and children. Some declared that the women always had plenty of money for their projects, while the general work starved. It was frequently stated that if there were only one organization at home base and abroad everything might then be kept in proper balance. The most unfair complaint was the charge that the women did not pay their share of basic mission work, which had to be done before there could be special activities for women and children. Actually the women were loyal supporters of general denominational budgets, and they went "a second mile" in raising funds for their special interests. Moreover they adjusted in the main to the general field program abroad.

Something that irked the leadership of the general church boards was the relatively low cost of administration and maintenance of the women's work, because they themselves were constantly under unfair attack regarding costs. Odious comparisons were made. The low cost of women's work was achieved principally through two factors. The first was the voluntary basis of the work. The second was the low salaries coupled with the remarkable devotion of the single women missionaries. All missionaries were supposed to serve sacrificially, but women missionaries generally existed on mere subsistence salaries. The women's societies and their Federation operated on "shoestring budgets." Almost all officers including executive secretaries were unpaid volunteers. A vast army of women at headquarters, in branch societies, and local auxiliaries all across the land found in this cause the grand passion of their lives. They unstintingly devoted time, energy, and abilities far beyond what might be reasonable expectations. It was all highly amateurish and unprofessional. It did create involvement of individuals.

Volunteer service kept home-base costs low. Maintenance costs were also low because it required far less to support an ill-paid single woman than a family. Retirement programs were often most unjust. The women's boards are open to the charge of exploitation of devoted missionaries. While Protestant women disliked the imposition of celibacy and poverty on Roman Catholic missionaries, male and female, they insisted almost as rigidly upon a similar requirement for their own staff. The whole women's missionary movement was built upon a celibate order of life-career missionaries maintained on a subsistence level. Women missionaries were expected to serve for life without ever getting married. Not even furlough was promised by the independent women's boards at the beginning, but they eventually came to adopt the practice. The result of this system was the most inexpensive missionary service possible for Protestants. Should a woman marry or resign before the end of her first term she was required, by a signed pledge, to return her travel and outfit allowance and sometimes her salary. The general boards similarly expected the return of the allowances in the case of early retirement, but marriage was no problem. An unwritten agreement among boards and societies, known as "comity in missionary marriage," required that the husband's board repay the wife's board for her expenses. But the officers of the women's boards were most unhappy about even intramission marriages. It is related that the secretary of the Woman's Board of Missions once went into the office of the foreign secretary of the American Board in great agitation, and told him that two missionaries under these Congregationalist boards announced their intention to marry. She asked: "What can we do?" The man replied that there was probably nothing that could be done except give a blessing, since marriage is a far older human institution than a missionary society. On one occasion in Egypt the women's society required a bridegroom to repay his bride's outfit and travel expenses within just a few days of the end of her first term. There are dozens of instances when young women were practically accused of being unfaithful to Christ as well as to the society because of marriage. Yet the bond of love and fellowship was far more intimate between the single women on the field and the women who supported them at home than between the missionaries of the general boards and the churches.

All this explains why the general boards' officers were often irked by the employment practices of the women's boards and irritated by comparison of costs. And, to be honest, there was sometimes a basis to the masculine complaint that women were interested only in their specialized work and did not understand mission problems as a whole. The reason for lack of concern, if it were true, was, of course, the exclusion of the women from participation in the basic program. Whatever the reasons and their worth, men pressed vigorously for integration. Commission Six of the World Missionary Conference at Edinburgh in 1910 asked whether the time had not arrived for merger or at least close association, and the members of the Foreign Missions Conference of North America continued thereafter to debate the subject.[1] Increasing pressure for integration was also exerted through denominational channels.

Mrs. Helen B. Montgomery often told the men that women would go far in cooperation or even merger, but would never consent to being mere collectors of funds for men to spend. Modern educated women not only have ideas about how to raise money, but also for what and how to spend it. The proposal of integration into one great board combining men and women sounds reasonable, but, she asked, "are men ready for it — are they emancipated from the caste of sex so that they can work easily with women, unless they be the head and women clearly subordinate?" What could women possibly expect from the men except the appointment of two or three women to some unimportant committee? Consolidated promotion of causes certainly had not been successful up to this time, and under merger work for women and children would surely be neglected. Women are far more diverse than men, have a distinctively feminine viewpoint, and they are interested in certain experiments that do not appeal to men. She affirmed that women's boards still have a distinctive contribution to make. The best solution, according to the champion of the women's missionary movement, would be to develop a distinctive and powerful laymen's missionary movement parallel to the female enterprise. Then "when the main lead is uncovered, the brethren will be too busy with their pickaxes mining the glittering veins of gold to grudge women their nuggets picked off the surface." Once, she told the men that it was a matter of democracy, which they did not practice with respect to women.[2]

Mrs. F. H. Sheets prepared an address for the 1917 meeting of the Foreign Missions Conference, but it was read by her husband. She told the men the two secrets of women's

[1] *World Missionary Conference, Edinburgh, 1910,* VI, 222-234; Foreign Mission Conference of N. A., *Annual Report, 1912* and *1917.*

[2] Helen B. Montgomery, *Western Women in Eastern Lands,* pp. 263-272; Foreign Missions Conference, *Annual Report, 1917,* pp. 139-151.

work. The women's societies had been successful because they had given women responsibility which nurtured Christian character, and had enlisted vast numbers of them through auxiliaries in genuine involvement — in intercession, service, and giving. She told the men frankly: "Any adjustments which fail to take into account this fact and fail to leave on the women an apparently overwhelming burden of responsibility, or do not delegate to them sufficient administrative initiative to nerve them to their greatest endeavor, will be in danger of defeating the very ends for which they are made."

The Edinburgh Conference's suggestion of a denominational joint committee of reference and counsel offered no solution to the Americans, because the general and women's boards already had established means of consultation and cooperation. Integration was what the men wanted. Eventually the women accepted the invitations or responded to pressures. This was in part because of denominational loyalty, and in part because of assurance that the causes for which they worked would be conserved. Integration began in the Methodist Church, South, and gradually took place in the other denominations, being generally completed by the end of the 1920s, but not being achieved in certain instances until 1956 and 1966. The story of the many mergers and adjustments cannot be related in detail. The Methodist, Congregational, Baptist, and Presbyterian cases will be briefly narrated.

The Methodist Episcopal Church, South, unified its entire missionary structure, effective in 1910. The two general and two women's boards of home and foreign missions were merged into a single Board of Missions. Within that Board there was a Women's Council responsible for home-base cultivation of women's interests. Women were given membership and secretarial posts supposedly in equal proportion to men. Dr. E. F. Cook and Mrs. J. B. Cobb were the foreign secretaries. There were also two educational secretaries, and a woman was editorial secretary. Dr. Rawlings at the 1912 meeting of the Foreign Missions Conference reported that the women held the balance of power and were using it well. Integration, he said, was mutually advantageous.[3]

The National Council of the Congregational Churches in 1924 politely but firmly coerced the three Woman's Boards of Missions to merge with the American Board by appointing a Committee on Missionary Organizations to achieve organizational unity on the grounds of improving efficiency. By May, 1925, the four boards had worked out a plan of union, which was adopted by the National Council the following October. Women would be added to the membership of the ABCFM Prudential Committee to the extent of at least one-third its total number, and secretaries would be of both sexes. Women's work on the fields would remain temporarily under women secretaries pending gradual integration. Headquarters of the women's boards would be closed, and American Board regional offices would take over their functions. Three boards voted approval by the end of 1925 and the Woman's Board of the Pacific did so in the following January. The Prudential Committee first met with women members on March 16, 1926, and formal consummation of the union was effected January 1, 1927.[4]

By that time the Presbyterians had already consolidated. The six separate women's boards long had a Central Committee, but it became much more effective in 1917 when it got an executive secretary. Since the Philadelphia, New York, and Chicago Societies were to celebrate their fiftieth anniversaries in 1920, all six resolved to join in a jubilee campaign of commemoration, which achieved far more than the goals set, including 198 new missionaries rather than the one hundred sought. The climax of the celebration was arranged in connection with the General Assembly in Philadelphia. Meanwhile, working together so intimately had led to merger of the six societies, and a new united Woman's Board of Foreign Missions was inaugurated at the Jubilee. Headquarters were established in New York in the same

---

[3] Foreign Missions Conference, *Annual Report, 1912*, p. 48.
[4] American Board of Commissioners for Foreign Missions, "Story of the Unification of the Boards," leaflet, 1926.

building with the denominational Board of Foreign Missions, and there the executive secretaries, Mrs. Charles K. Roys and Miss Gertrude Schultz, entered into good relations with their men neighbors. Both boards were satisfied with the arrangement, but only two years later the General Assembly of 1922, without consulting the membership or executives of either board, voted to merge the two agencies. Fifteen out of forty members of the Board were to be women, the executive secretaries of the Woman's Board were given posts, and it was intended that in this manner women should have a direct influence in the whole enterprise of foreign mission. A special department of women's work sought to conserve and develop the existing women's organizations on synodical, presbyterial, and congregational levels. Therefore, involvement and interest on the part of women were maintained more successfully than in some other churches. Yet Dr. Arthur J. Brown could comment in later years: "Whether the consolidation of the Woman's Board with the Assembly's Board has resulted in more and better work by women is not clear. . . . But the whole foreign missionary work for women ceased to have the freedom of action that it had hitherto possessed and came under ecclesiastical control as an integral part of the official foreign missionary agency of the Church."[5]

The Baptist story is quite different from the two cases just related. The women's work moved from a subordinate to a coordinate position and then was integrated with the denominational general society by a very simple device. The two regional women's foreign missionary societies united in 1913-14, and the Woman's American Baptist Foreign Mission Society was recognized as an agency of the Northern Baptist Convention in 1914. A Joint Council of the A.B.F.M.S. and the Woman's A.B.F.M.S. was created in 1915. The two societies engaged in a number of joint projects over the subsequent years, such as the Lone Star Fund and the Judson Fund. In some inexplicable manner there was adopted in 1929 a new basis of cooperation which recognized the sov-

---

[5] Arthur J. Brown, *One Hundred Years*, pp. 138-143.

ereignty and independence of the W.A.B.F.M.S. in women's work. There developed in the Convention a growing desire for integration, but the women resisted it until 1941 when a joint committee favored merger. However, the War brought too many problems to allow time for pursuit of this recommendation, although a temporary wartime Cabinet, composed of representatives from both, was empowered to exercise all functions of the two boards. The historian of the Baptist mission, Robert G. Torbet, judges that at the end of the War the Woman's Society in relation to the A.B.F.M.S. was in a position more equal than ever before.

A decade passed before the Convention pressed for integration. Then the two societies in 1954 adopted a plan which was reported to both the two Societies and the American (formerly Northern) Baptist Convention in May, 1955. Integration was voted on on May 19 and achieved by the simple means of each society electing a Board of Managers with identical membership. Departments and secretarial assignments were adjusted. The new joint Board of Managers consisted of twenty-eight men and thirty-two women, with Mrs. Frank C. Wigginton as chairman. The first and second vicepresidents were women, and seven (of fifteen) committee and subcommittee chairmanships were held by women. The general secretary and directors of the two major departments were men, but women held important administrative posts. Thus Miss Hazel F. Shank administered Burma and Thailand, and Mrs. Charles H. Sears Japan, the Philippines, and Hong Kong. A subcommittee on Work for Women and Children was provided.[6] What appears full parity in the beginning has not been retained by the women in later years.

The case of the Methodist women is most interesting, because they kept their independence longer than others. The Methodist Episcopal Church, the Methodist Episcopal

---

[6] Mrs. Henry G. Safford, *The Golden Jubilee*, p. 172; Robert G. Torbet, *Venture of Faith*, pp. 179, 399, 414-415, 417, 423, 429, 453; American Baptist F.M.S. and W.A.B.F.M.S., *Along Kingdom Highways, Annual Report, 1955*, p. 27; *Missions*, CLIII, 1 (Jan. 1955), 55; no. 6 (June 1955), p. 22.

Church, South, and the Methodist Protestant Church united after long negotiations in 1939. The structure adopted for the Methodist Church united home and foreign missions under a single Board of Missions. It also brought the women's work of the three churches into one unit within the Board of Missions. This Woman's Division of Christian Service was related to the entire mission program of the church without destroying the independence and initiative formerly exercised by the Woman's Foreign Missionary Society of the Methodist Episcopal Church. This is most remarkable in view of the trends prevailing at that time and the strong central organization of the church. It is said to be due solely to the determined opposition of the women to attempted subordination and thorough integration. Valiant women carried their case even to the floor of the General Conference. It is related, for example, that on an occasion when Bishop Francis J. McConnell was presiding over a session dealing with the subject, Mrs. McConnell repeatedly sought to speak but could not get recognition. Finally someone called the attention of the Bishop to his wife. He remarked that he knew that voice and had been hearing it for many years. Thereupon Mrs. McConnell was permitted to speak and made a strong, effective presentation of the women's point of view.

The Board of Missions comprised three autonomous and incorporated administrative divisions, Home Missions, Foreign (later World) Missions, and the Woman's Division of Christian Service, plus a joint Division of Education and Cultivation to serve the three. Women were given equal representation with men apart from the bishops on the Board of Managers. The constitution (*Discipline,* 1939) gave the Woman's Division responsibility for all women's life, organization, and work at home and abroad. This included promotion and direction of societies on local, conference, and General Conference levels and actual planning, implementation, and administration of mission programs at home and overseas. The unification of the women's interests and activities was an enormous task, and the achievements of the Woman's Division during the next quarter-century are unequaled in other denominations. The program authorized by the constitution was stated in most sweeping terms:—

> to develop and maintain Christian work among women and children at home and abroad; to cultivate Christian family life; to enlist and organize the efforts of Christian women, young people, and children in behalf of native and foreign groups, needy childhood, and community welfare; to assist in the promotion of a missionary spirit throughout the Church; to select, train, and maintain Christian workers; to cooperate with the local Church in its responsibilities, and to seek fellowship with Christian women of this and other lands in establishing a Christian social order around the world.

What a charter! What a challenge! That statement sums up the entire scope and the goals of the American women's foreign missionary movement as it had developed during the previous eighty years.

One of the most centralized polities made room for women's independence and initiative. The Methodist Church gave its Woman's Division authority equal to the responsibility — far beyond what was allowed in other denominations. This included "authority to regulate its own proceedings; to select fields of labor; to accept, train, commission, and maintain workers; . . . to buy and sell property. . . ." The giving of the women's societies was channeled directly into the Division.[7]

The Woman's Division carried out its home and foreign programs through separate departments. Both these interests were promoted through the Woman's secretary of the joint Division of Education and Cultivation. Several means of liaison were provided between the units within the Board of Missions and between that agency and the Board of Education. There was likewise similar consultation between the foreign secretaries of the World and Woman's Divisions. An able team of women secretaries for overseas work — Miss Sallie Lou MacKinnon, Miss Elizabeth Lee, Mrs. Velma Maynor, and Mrs. Otis Moore — formed the counterpart of the ex-

---

[7] In addition to the *Discipline*, 1939 ed., see "Constitution and By-laws," in Woman's Division of Christian Service, *First Annual Report, 1940-41*, pp. 145-186.

cellent group of men secretaries under Dr. Ralph E. Diffendorfer. The women were responsible overseas chiefly for educational and medical institutions for women and for general women's and children's ministries. The schools and colleges for women in subsequent years were maintained at an unusually high level of quality at a time when Christian institutions generally tended to fall below the upgraded national schools.

Official documents seem to indicate that when reorganization was effected in 1964 it was the bishops who were bent on integration. The recurring word is "elimination of dual control." The Board of Missions began a study of its structure in January, 1963, and a plan of reorganization was adopted a year later. The General Conference of 1964 enacted the changes into law.[8] A general secretary and a full-time treasurer were added so as "to unify program and finances." The Foreign Department of the W.D.C.S. was merged with the World Division into the Division of International Missions. The Woman's Division, deprived of actual mission action at home and abroad, now carries on its work through departments of Program and Cultivation, Christian Social Relations, and Finance, and joins in joint departments for education and personnel purposes. The women have received what may appear to be excellent representation on the Board of Managers of the Division of International Missions, having twenty-nine representatives alongside nine ministers, nineteen laymen, three youths (one a girl), and ten domestic bishops and six overseas bishops. Yet both within and without Methodism it has been questioned whether any possible number of lay men and women can balance sixteen bishops. Area secretaries and executives of similar grade were supposed to be equally distributed between the sexes, but this was not quite achieved. But henceforth an area executive, be he man or woman, administered the total field program

---

8 *Journal of the 23rd Annual Meeting of the Methodist Church, Board of Missions, Jan. 8-17, 1963*, p. 30; *24th Annual Meeting, 1964*, pp. 68-72; General Conference, *Journal of the 1964 Gen. Conf.*, I, 422, 573-688, 893; "Questions and Answers to Restructuring of the Board of Missions of the Methodist Church," mimeographed, 1964.

and personnel. When the Methodist Church and the Evangelical United Brethren Church united to form the United Methodist Church, the structure for mission remained the same as the Methodist pattern with some change of names, for example, The Board of Global Mission, The World Division, The Home Mission Division, and the Women's Division of Christian Service.

The Woman's Division of Christian Service has continued its extensive and intensive program of education and promotion of the total mission. However, in the realm of action it of necessity must concentrate on homeland social service and relations. There are signs that it is this which is now coming to mean *mission* to the women of the church, although this is only part of mission, albeit that part in which the women of Methodism can still be directly involved.

There was integration in the realm of interdenominational cooperation as well as in the denominations. It was in 1912 that the Foreign Missions Conference of North America first permitted women to be included in a general board's delegation if the budget of the women's society were included in the general budget figure for purposes of representation. Independent women's societies might have direct membership. This move was made over the vigorous objection of a certain secretary who argued that the presence of women delegates would drastically change the character of the Conference and prevent freedom of discussion. Women would put an end to the old fellowship. Twenty regular women members and twenty other women attended the next session in 1913. The W.F.M.S. of the Methodist Church was now a member and two nondenominational societies were represented. For the first time a woman was appointed to committee membership. Women were now permanently part of the F.M.C.

A further step was taken in 1915 when the Committee of Reference and Council was empowered to co-opt both men and women as members of its subcommittees, and the following year Mrs. Henry W. Peabody and Miss Margaret E. Hodge were elected to that executive organ. From that year onward the F.M.C. *Annual Report* carried a directory of women's boards. The F.M.C. and the Federation of Woman's Boards became increasingly involved in joint cooperative enterprises, such as the Board of Missionary Preparation and the Joint Committee of Conference, which sought to coordinate mission study. Topics relating to women's work were frequently included in the annual programs. Women as well as men were included in memorial minutes. A woman was usually elected vice-chairman of the annual meeting, and in 1930 Helen B. Calder was the first woman chairman. Men and women came increasingly to learn to work together.[9]

The Committee of Reference and Counsel in 1931 began a study aimed at improving the efficiency of the Foreign Missions Conference in its services to member boards. The Conference of 1932 gave the Committee power to effect changes in organization. The Federation of Woman's Boards of Foreign Missions was invited to explore possibilities of closer association, with the consequence that a joint committee recommended merger of the two organizations, in which all essential interests of both would be retained, secretarial posts would be open to women, and a genuine partnership of men and women would be effected. The F.M.C. approved the plan in 1932, and, although there was not unanimity, the Federation also approved, and the merger was consummated.[10]

There was added to the Conference structure a Committee of Women's Work responsible for cooperation with independent women's organizations, for promotion of the World Day of Prayer jointly with the Home Mission agency, and above all for cultivation of the three union activities so long especially dear to the women — Christian literature, union women's colleges, and mission study. The Federation secretary, Miss Florence G. Tyler, joined Dr. Leslie B. Moss as

---

[9] Foreign Missions Conference of N. A., *Annual Report, 1912*, pp. 30-31, 46-48, 150-151; *1913*, pp. 9-14, 191-201; *1915*, pp. 48-49; *1916*, pp. 25-30, 272-275; *1917*, pp. 139-151; *1919*, pp. 247-275; *1921*, pp. 126-146.

[10] Federation of Woman's Boards of Foreign Missions, *Annual Report, 1933*, "Minutes of Administrative Committee," pp. 6-7; "Minutes of Annual Conference," p. 4; and appended "Report of Committee on Integration"; Foreign Missions Conference of N. A., *Annual Report, 1932*, pp. 9, 13; *1933*, pp. 12, 13; *1934*, pp. 16, 34, 47-52.

an executive of the F.M.C. All member boards of the Federation were now members of the Conference. The Committee on Christian Literature for Women and Children and the United Committee for the Study of Missions were offered membership, but the latter surrendered responsibility for the production of study books and aids to the Missionary Education Movement, terminated its existence, and gave to the Committee on Women's Work the balance in its treasury.[11] The Committee on Women's Work, served by the woman executive of the Conference, related mission interests abroad to home missions and the United Council of Church Women through liaison agencies, and was one of the three sponsors of *The Church Woman*. When Florence G. Tyler retired at the end of 1941 she was succeeded by Miss Sue E. Weddell, then general secretary of the Reformed Church Women's Board. She shared with Dr. Emory Ross executive responsibility for the multiplying area and functional committees — India, for example, being her portfolio — but was especially charged with all women's special concerns.[12]

Through these years the women's interchurch movement was gaining strength through the leadership of the National Council of Church Women. It sought to foster the commitment of women to unity locally and to combine the old interest in home and foreign missions with social service and action. The complicated story of developments cannot be reviewed here, and readers are referred to *Follow These Women* by Gladys G. Calkins. The Council of Women for Home Missions meanwhile had merged with the Home Missions Council. Women executives and associated leaders in the two interdenominational mission agencies and in the individual boards were deeply involved in the evolving movement of churchwomen in unity and service. The national women's agency was reorganized in 1941 at a convention in Atlantic City as the United Council of Church Women. Its purpose was stated to be "to unite church women in their allegiance to their Lord and Savior Jesus Christ, through

11 Foreign Missions Conference, *Annual Report, 1934*, pp. 16, 47-52; *1939*, p. 113.

12 *Ibid., 1934-1935;* and files of the Committee on Women's Work in the Division of Overseas Ministries, National Council of Churches.

a program looking to their integration in the total life and work of the church, and to the upbuilding of a world Christian community." The U.C.C.W. correlated more than 1,500 local interchurch women's societies or councils, and claimed to represent ten million women in seventy denominations. Mrs. Ruth M. Worrell became executive secretary. The original dynamic of overseas missions, which had produced the local interchurch union societies, plus the somewhat later and lesser force of home mission concerns, were now diluted, but not lost, in a multifaceted interest in total Christian witness.[13]

When the United Council of Church Women became fully functioning, the Foreign Mission Conference's Committee on Women's Work dissolved, because almost all its former functions and responsibilities were now being discharged by U.C.C.W. It was replaced by a continuation committee called Special Program and Funds, which was expected to keep women's interests before the Conference and member boards, arrange an occasional special conference, and carry certain responsibilities for the World Day of Prayer. This committee nominated fifteen members to the Board of the U.C.C.W. so as to assure a continuing overseas mission interest, contributed articles to *The Church Woman,* and arranged visits of women from the younger churches in the United States. Further interaction and stimulation resulted from the creation of the Department of World Missions in U.C.C.W. and the appointment of Mrs. James A. Evans as director. She was deeply involved in the work of the Foreign and Home Mission agencies.[14]

The Foreign Missions Conference, Home Missions Council, Federal Council of Churches, and a dozen other cooperative interdenominational agencies merged in 1950 into the

---

[13] Gladys G. Calkins, *Follow These Women, Church Women in the Ecumenical Movement.*

[14] Foreign Missions Conference, *Annual Report, 1942,* p. 82; Division of Foreign Missions, *Annual Report, 1950,* Report of the Committee on Special Program and Funds; records of the Committee on Special Program and Funds, in Division of Overseas Ministries.

National Council of Churches. The F.M.C. became the Division of Foreign Missions, and is now known as the Division of Overseas Ministries. The United Council of Church Women became the General Department of United Church Women. As long as there was a woman associate general secretary in the Division of Overseas Ministries there continued to be a recognized and definitely located responsibility for women's work and interests, to some degree at least; but that last structural vestige of the old Federation of Woman's Boards of Foreign Missions vanished in 1966.[15] The special literature work for women and children is the one long-time major activity of the Federation that is still carried on through the Division. The Committee on Christian Literature for Women and Children in Mission Fields still retains its legal corporate existence, but functions through the D.O.M. Committee on Christian Literature and World Literacy.

This literature program continued to stress the production of magazines. Nine new ones were added between 1943 and 1951, including the important *Christian Home Magazine* in India. More and more national editors took over this work from missionaries. The magazines circulated extensively, had many readers per copy, and were generally more effective than books as mass media. Miss Weddell reports a comment of Miss Clementina Butler, long-time chairman of the Committee: "Instead of putting books on our shelves and selling them one by one, the cost of a book will send a magazine twelve times a year right into the home. Are we not wise to let the post-office system do this important part of our work for us? We might call the village post box an unrecognized bearer of the good news of the Kingdom." From 1913 to 1958 the Committee invested $623,355 in production of magazines. As income increased support of other new projects was also undertaken, including Braille translations for Korean blind children, Sunday school curriculum material,

---

15 National Council of the Churches of Christ, Division of Foreign Missions, Division of World Missions, Division of Overseas Ministries, *Annual Reports, 1950-1966;* files of the Committee on Women's Work and Committee on Special Program and Funds, 1950-1966.

bookmobiles and book fairs, home and family-life publications, reading for children in wartime, supplying paper stock for printing, and the training of national writers and editors. Increasingly the funds for all this activity from the early 1930s onward came from World Day of Prayer offerings. Meanwhile, literature work, which had been scattered in many quarters, and literacy education, which got its great original impetus from Dr. Frank C. Laubach, had been united in the Committee on Christian Literature and World Literacy or the "Lit-Lit Committee," as it is popularly known. The Christian Literature Committee, guided by the women's work secretary of the Division of Overseas Ministries (then D.F.M.), cooperated more and more closely with Lit-Lit. It was a logical move in 1957 to bring its operations entirely within the Lit-Lit structure and program. The Doane bequest and World Day of Prayer offerings made it possible to expand this special program under professional administration. Miss Marion Van Horne joined the staff of Lit-Lit in 1957 with this portfolio, and a joint committee was created for responsible direction. This is one instance in which integration brought more adequate professional service, and expanded and improved the quality of a major activity of the former women's boards of foreign missions.[16]

World Day of Prayer offerings financed this continuing literature work for women and children and also provided annual contributions to a number of the union women's colleges abroad. World Day of Prayer symbolized the unity and totality of the Christian mission in a growing realization of a worldwide Christian community. As the distinctive women's foreign missionary organizations passed, this Day seems in the decades of the thirties and early forties to have given many women their chief means of involvement in world mission, although the Christian fellowship aspect of it loomed ever larger. As in the past, the greatest emphasis was put on intercession, and the offerings were in a sense but the manifestation of the genuineness of the prayers. It was the

---

16 Sue Weddell, *More Than Paper and Ink*, pp. 25-33.

one remaining means by which all women could inter-
denominationally still participate in those long-standing concerns of the past. Even when every allowance is made for
inflation and the steady decline in the value of the dollar,
the increase in the annual offerings is significant. This is
especially true of the war years, when Christian love and
mutual concern could be expressed in this manner despite
broken fellowship and disrupted programs. The U. S. A. offerings from 1934 to 1941 increased from $19,119 to $64,409.
During the war years through 1945 the offerings totalled
$84,820; $108,276; $144,671; and $184,336. After a brief decline to $175,388, there was a rise of $468,900 in 1955.

There is no more moving set of documents in recent
church history than the account of the previous year's observance sent out annually as background material for each
new Day. The statements reveal not only the multiplication
of services in this country but also the extension of the Day
as an ecumenical observance among Christian women everywhere. Thus the leaflet entitled "The Print of His Feet in
the Earth" on the 1941 Day brought hope in the midst of
the terrors of war in Europe and China. It told how despite
air raids there had been more meetings than ever in Britain,
with women being deeply moved by being part of such a
fellowship. In Shanghai eighteen different nationalities were
represented by women kneeling side by side, "with Chinese
beside Japanese, German beside English, Jew beside German."
The 1944 account reminded American women how they
were linked with their sisters in Australia, New Zealand,
and South Africa. Typical is this report from the Diocese
of the Arctic in Canada: "The Eskimo Women's Association
describes 'a very hearty service in the school, including also
every white woman in the settlement; beautiful program,
could not be improved upon; produced very deep reverence.
Service in Loucheaux, English, and Eskimo. Afternoon service for Technical School, 400 youth of every creed imaginable.
Best of all, they enjoyed it.' "

The planning and administration of the World Day of

Prayer is a complicated story. Sufficient it is to state that from 1928 it was the responsibility of the national women's interchurch organization under its various names, with the cooperation of the two interdenominational mission agencies. A central World Day of Prayer Committee was created in 1937 and chaired by Miss Margaret T. Applegarth through an entire decade. This committee planned and printed the program and distributed it with supporting material throughout the United States. The realm of "foreign relations" was the responsibility of the Committee on Women's Work of the Foreign Missions Conference and its successor, the Committee on Special Program and Funds of the Division of Overseas Ministries. This included enlistment of agencies to sponsor the observance in additional countries, all foreign correspondence, the sending of programs and material, and the transmission of gifts. Miss Weddell relates how each year when the packets were sent overseas a prayer meeting was held at the mail chute. Eventually this function was surrendered to the World Day of Prayer Committee of United Church Women, as was fitting and proper.

During the 1930s the offering was generally divided between migrant work and Indian schools as home mission activities and the union women's colleges and the Committee on Christian Literature for Women and Children as foreign mission objects. In 1937 the sum of $7,183 was given the eight women's colleges then assisted, and $6,785 to the Committee on Christian Literature. Twenty years later they received respectively $93,000 and $45,000. The colleges — some additional schools having been added — in the early 1960s generally received about $100,000. Emergency needs were great in the years following the end of World War II, and the World Day of Prayer gave the Committee on Special Program and Funds additional funds for such purposes. That Committee then regularly made grants to the Committee on Friendly Relations with Foreign Students and to special projects of the International Missionary Council. In the '60s the training of women leaders in the young churches was aided substantially.[17]

Note should be taken in this brief summary of the World Day of Prayer of its seventy-fifth anniversary in 1962 and of the internationalizing of its administration. A large special committee planned the celebration and Miss Sue Weddell wrote the program for the Day. The major feature of the anniversary was the sponsoring of thirty-seven Prayer Fellowships across the country and in various parts of the world. Teams of American churchwomen joined women from wide areas in a number of locations, and these groups engaged in prayer and consultation about the total mission of the church in the world. The East Asian Prayer Fellowship at Hong Kong brought together women from the countries of the region plus a few from Australia, Samoa, and Madagascar. Women of southern Asia and the Middle East gathered at Madras. To the Ecumenical Center at Mindolo, Zambia, came women from the nations of Africa. Zurich was the meeting place of European women from both sides of the Iron Curtain. There was a Latin America Prayer Fellowship, too. Summary accounts of the Fellowship were circulated and some printed in *The Church Woman*. The meetings greatly strengthened the sense of the universality and unity of the church of Christ, stimulated extension of the observance, and dramatized to American churchwomen the fruits of that mission to and for women to which their mothers and grandmothers had given so great devotion. The attendance, fervor, and offerings clearly showed the impact of this unusual preparation.[18]

It was frequently said by leaders of the World Day of Prayer observance during the past quarter-century that the administration of what had become a universal enterprise

---

17 Files of the Committees on Women's Work and Special Program and Funds through 1966; Ruth M. Worrell, *The Day Thou Gavest*, pp. 8-43; Florence Gordon, "The World Day of Prayer," *International Review of Missions*, July 1949.

18 "World Day of Prayer, 75th Anniversary, Report of Prayer Fellowships, 1961," mimeographed; *The Church Woman*, June-July 1961.

ought to be internationalized. It happened that a goodly number of women connected with various national World Day of Prayer committees were to be in the United States in 1967. Others were invited if possible to join them in a conference at Anderson College, Anderson, Indiana, from June 6 to 11. An *ad hoc* international committee and staff planned and guided the conference. The women made general plans for future planning and administration. A provisional committee was selected with Mrs. Rathie Selvaratnam as chairman. This committee has called a conference of official delegates of the national committees to meet in Sweden in the summer of 1968. The permanent working committee when established will meet in various parts of the world so as to permit national groups in the several regions better to participate.

The structures have been traced through which American women participated in the Protestant world mission from 1800 to the dissolution of the women's boards of foreign missions. Something has been narrated about home-base and field action. Integration of the women's societies into the denominational boards took place between 1910 and 1964, but was generally achieved by the end of the 1920s. Two studies should now be made of the last forty years, one being an investigation of women's actual participation in world mission through the present denominational structures, the other a survey of work for women and children overseas. Then there would be a solid vantage point from which to evaluate the enterprise carried on through the old women's boards. Neither study can be made for this book. But the record set forth in this book should be evaluated from the perspective of the present situation, and the contemporary situation may profitably be analyzed from the viewpoint of the achievements of the women's foreign missionary movement. Up to this point every aspect of the story has been thoroughly documented; but now the writer must turn from historical method to the technique of the surveyor and reporter, basing his interpretation on interviews and on his own personal participation in organized world mission during the past thirty-odd years. These interviews have been sufficiently numerous to provide a fair sample, and they include laywomen presently or formerly active in overseas missions and women who have served or are serving professionally as executives in denominational and ecumenical agencies. Fewer men have been specifically consulted on this subject.

There are two factors in the overseas work of the American churches which raise questions at this point. One is the alarming decrease in the proportion of single women on the missionary staff. Today there are not enough recruits to fill vacancies, and there is a growing disposition on the part of those who volunteer to seek short-term service rather than a life career. North American single women missionaries numbered 4,824 in 1925. Adding the figures reported for each board in the Missionary Research Library's 1966 *Directory of North American Protestant Foreign Mission Agencies,* the figure of 4,828 is found. This includes a large number of short-term workers, who were few in 1925. Meanwhile the entire American staff has increased from 13,555 to over 28,000. The proportion of single women to the whole is decidedly less.

A number of factors are probably responsible for this decrease in vocations. There is the general apathy about mission in the churches and suspicion about the rightness of sending missionaries abroad to seek the conversion of other peoples. But the churches are quite ready to engage in interchurch aid with personnel and funds. Another factor is contemporary youth's lack of interest in religion and especially in the church. Also skepticism about missions is widespread among students, and they hold to an outmoded stereotype of the missionary. Another cause is probably the slowness with which mission boards have opened new types of service to women, and to that we shall return. A very important factor is certainly the multiplication of opportunities for overseas service under nonchurch agencies — American and foreign governments, the Peace Corps especially, business, and a variety of voluntary agencies. Still another factor is the present social pressure for a girl to marry young. But after taking all these into account, the present writer believes that the most potent factor has been the termination of a distinctive women's missionary movement carried out through women's agencies. After the end of intense cultivation by women voluntarily enlisted in the work of the women's foreign boards, girls have not been "brought up in the mission" as were their mothers and have not had the challenge of vocation held constantly before them. The nondenominational missionary societies, whose supporting constituencies are still intensely involved personally, do not have the recruiting problems of the church boards.

If the women's boards had continued independent existence, would they have moved into new lines of service and given more opportunity for women with special talents and interests who have in recent years gone abroad under other agencies? That question cannot be answered with any assurance. But it can be said that the women's boards put personnel into areas of distinct need and that they were highly experimental in earlier times. Their spokesmen often claimed that women were indeed highly experimental in policy and strategy and far more ready than men to take a risk. Doubtless the pressures from established institutions would have continued assignment of the largest portion of the staff to education and medicine; but the women's boards, relating to national women more directly than to churches, might well have been more free than the general boards — which have limited themselves more and more to responding to requests from young church officials — to put more personnel into new types of ministry.

At the home base, integration and the elimination of dual administration, so urgently desired by denominational officials, have been completely attained. Have they been bought at too great a price? The majority of women interviewed say, Yes! Moreover, has the spirit of the promises made to the women been kept, no matter what may be said about the letter? The majority of women who have kept their major concern for world mission believe that women have less and less a place of genuine influence and participation in administrative offices, board membership, and policy-making. They believe that women have seldom been given executive posts in equal measure with men in either denominational or ecumenical organizations. Often when the question is raised men have a strange way of counting noses. They will enumerate the second- and third-line posts held by women — even routine secretarial or clerical jobs — and compare this total with the number of men in policy-exercising positions. Furthermore, they point to the fact that the number of women in high executive posts continues to decline. When a woman executive retires, the position is all too seldom filled by another woman. It is often said, quite properly, "We shall not bring sex into the choice, but call the best-qualified person." It is amazing that so seldom is this best-qualified person a woman! It is most rare for a man to be succeeded by a woman. A woman's peculiar gifts are lost in the direction of world mission in consequence of her progressive exclusion — the power of heart as well as intellect, the important feminine intuition, her impatience with bureaucratic procrastination and endless discussion before action, and her readiness in faith and hope to take a risk. A number of talented women have reported that they have refused positions because, on the one hand, they would not be fully accepted on the basis of merit, nor, on the other, be permitted truly to represent the woman's point of view. They felt that they would be expected to be "an organization man."

However, the big problem is that of personal and congregational commitment, involvement, and participation in world mission. The greatest loss consequent to the end of the distinctive, organized women's world mission movement has been the decline of missionary dynamism and zeal in the churches. There is a multiplicity of causes behind the lack of interest of American Christians in world missions, to be sure. It is due in large part to the secularization of society, to the dilution of faith, to the questioning of the rightness of seeking conversions among persons of other religions, and to the great confusion about what mission should be in the time of a worldwide Christian community. It is further due in considerable measure to current ideas that mission is for the individual merely "Christian presence," and that for the congregation, national denomination, and Christian community at large, mission is the confrontation of society with the gospel just where they happen to exist. This is mission indeed, or the church's apostolate; and it is encouraging to see in our country new zeal for witness to men in our industrial, urban culture. But the "sending" half of the apostolate is largely forgotten or actually denied having validity. Nevertheless, throughout the history of the church it has been the "foreign" mission that kept alive devotion to the apostolate, and in modern times both "home missions" and stewardship were essentially products of the mission to the nations. As to world-mission interest, many point to the fact that never before have so many persons given so much as today. But that giving is largely a reflection of American economic prosperity and is the product of denominational budgetary centralization, promotion by a single department of stewardship and cultivation, and the apportionment system. All denominational causes are lumped together. More individuals give now, but it appears that this giving is to far too great an extent without commitment, prayer, and involvement. Recalling what happened to foreign-mission giving in the depression years, one may fear the collapse of the system should economic hard times come again. Continuing, sacrificial giving can be assured only by actual personal involvement and participation. Never since the decade of 1810 to 1820 has commitment to world mission been so low in our Protestant churches.

The author concludes that this lack of concern and involvement is in large measure due to the decline of women's direct participation. From the Civil War to the 1920s it was chiefly women who enlisted the forces of the church in world mission and to alien groups in the homeland. They did it through volunteer, not professional or ecclesiastical, participation in the enterprise. There was an immediate connection between the local churchwoman and the overseas work. The passionate devotion of the women was directed to communication of the gospel to women and girls, to liberating them socially by its power, and to enlisting new Christian women in the same cause in their turn. Now, however, the "sending" is as remote to most women as to the men. The women educated themselves, girls, and children in missions, and to a great extent influenced sweethearts, husbands, fathers, sons, and men acquaintances. When direct participation, education, and promotion were taken from them and they were no longer asked to do the seemingly impossible, passionate devotion cooled. Only where denominational mission boards were able to continue cultivation of women's societies and to ask them for extra gifts, has the level of contributions been maintained or increased. Centralized promotion and stewardship cultivation have seldom produced passionate devotion to mission. This comes only by contagion from person to person. Given commitment and zeal, then education and promotion can cultivate and illumine devotion.

Mission has become a plant root-bound in the ecclesiastical pots to which it is now confined — denominational and ecumenical structures. These organizations frown upon spontaneous action and establishment of direct relationships which they do not initiate or administer. Structures allow less and less personal and congregational involvement, and consequently lay men and women are increasingly participating in extra-ecclesiastical interdenominational and international agencies. The so-called "faith missions" grow in strength. They can live only on personal commitment and involvement. The apparent consequences of the destruction of the women's foreign missionary movement seems to support the thesis of Canon Max Warren in England, Professor Hans-Werner Gensichen, and others in Europe that the voluntary principle is essential to world mission. The prevailing American view has been that mission is the function of the church and must be discharged by an official denominational board. There is good theological foundation for that view. The primary function of the church is witness. But boards never enlisted a larger percentage of church members in actual involvement in world mission than did societies. It might well be recalled that the great architect of American world mission, Rufus Anderson, taught that a mission board exists only in order to enable missionaries and disciples in the churches to discharge their personal obedience to the Great Commission which our Lord has directed to them personally. The lesson that seems to emerge from the consequences of integration appears to be that denominational boards ought to find within their structure and program a large place for voluntary participation in such a manner as to involve the individual disciple and local congregation intimately in the work and relationships to which the structure is directed.

One more feature of the former women's missionary movement should be noted. It was composed of denominational societies or boards through which the women worked voluntarily, but these women were consciously engaged in one single world missionary enterprise. It was characterized by united action and was both symbolized and nurtured by an ecumenical organ, the Federation of Woman's Boards of Foreign Missions. It was from the beginning an interchurch movement. Out of its grass-roots vitality came the later United Church Women. No matter what denominational boards may do in the future to involve their women more directly and intimately in their work, it seems clear from past experience that women want an ecumenical organ to give cohesion and direction to their whole enterprise. It can no longer be a purely "foreign" or "home" mission cooperative agency, but must be concerned with every phase and aspect of the one world mission of the church of Christ to all the world. The experience of the past and a survey in the present indicate that the women want and need a free agency for fellowship, thinking, and action. They do not want to be shackled by rigid ecumenical structures any more than by denominational ones.

The transformation of United Church Women into Church Women United is a hopeful and promising move toward such freedom in unity. A tie with the National Council of Churches is retained through a Department of Women's Relations committee in the Division of Christian Unity, prepared to work with other departments of that Division such as those for youth and councils of churches. But Church Women United is now a free "visible fellowship to witness to [Christian women's] faith in Jesus Christ as divine Lord and Savior and, enabled by His Spirit, go out together into every neighborhood and nation as instruments of His reconciling love." Worldwide ecumenical fellowship and "Intercontinental Mission" have as large a place as mission to American society and culture. Church Women United know that they are living in one world to which there is one mission of the church of Christ, and that the frontiers beyond our borders are not to be forgotten. The Intercontinental Mission budget will receive its funds primarily from the World Day of Prayer, May Fellowship Day, and World Community Day, but these offerings have been made "open-ended" so that individuals may contribute at will. An emergency service, called "Neighbors Now," is maintained ready to meet suddenly appearing needs, such as the plight of victims of war in the Middle East in 1967. Another international program is named "Christian Causeways." It is a program by which American churchwomen involve themselves in mutual service and consultation on fundamental issues with women in other parts of the world. The 1968/69 field for interchange of teams was Latin America.

It appears that Church Women United may provide for the women executives and women lay leaders of the denominations a highly desirable means of joint study and discussion. The Executive Staff Conference which brings together the denominational women secretaries has been strengthened primarily "to coordinate and encourage study and action programs which interpret the mission of the church." On the point of personal involvement Miss Margaret Shannon, Director of the Church Women United, stated: "Taking into account the growing number of employed women, plans for individual participation in ecumenical mission were developed." And she summarizes the 1966/67 developments in these words: "Thus in ways appropriate to the times in which they live, the renewal of a movement with a mission was begun."

This survey of the American Protestant women's world missionary movement began with a Cent Society and a woman's mite. The object of that movement was to carry the gospel to women all over the world, and, when they had been transformed by that gospel, to enlist them in that same mission of proclamation and liberation, confident that they would give it new power and probably new direction. Christian women in Asia, Africa, and other regions are answering those expectations. It is fitting that in recognition of the fulfillment of this hope this book should report a contemporary reference to a woman's mite and its new promise of power in mission.

Out of Asia has arisen the Fellowship of the Least Coin. An Indian woman with the beautiful name of Shanti or Peace — Shanti Solomon — traveled in East Asia in the autumn of 1956 as a member of a fellowship team engaged in Bible study with women of the region. She had to remain in the Philippines while her teammates went to Korea because of visa restrictions. She thought: few can travel, but all Christian women should cultivate sisterhood in Christ's worldwide family. She sought an act of remembrance that might engage women, however isolated they might be, in prayer for all peoples and enlist them as "ministers of reconciliation in a world of barriers and broken fellowship." Shanti Solomon sought a tangible token of such sharing in universal fellowship of prayer which each and every woman, rich or poor, or of any class or status, might be able to give. In a flash of insight the answer came to her. It would be "the least coin" of any country, given once a month. This would not be a means of raising money or a form of stewardship, but a token of involvement in a fellowship of intercession and reconciliation.

The Philippine women eagerly adopted the proposal, and within ten years the Fellowship came to have a membership on every continent and in most countries. The Asian Church Women's Conference at Hong Kong in 1958 recommended that the women of each country decide how the money collected should be used. At the second conference in Thailand in 1962 it was decided to stimulate the spiritual nature of the Fellowship by distributing a prayer booklet, which was to be prepared by Hong Kong women. The third three-year *Circle of Prayer* is now in wide use. The secretary of the Asian Church Women's Conference, Mrs. Bautista of the Philippines, came to the United States in 1966 and urged Church Women United to enlist all American churchwomen in the Fellowship. The Board of Managers gladly commended it to the membership and to all Christian women. Despite the fact that raising money is never stressed and the amount of national offerings is never announced, the least coins added up to the equivalent of a half-million American dollars in ten years. These funds have been devoted always to a wide variety of mission projects in all parts of the world.

VIII

THE DECADE OF THE SEVENTIES

THE DECADE SINCE THIS BOOK WAS FIRST PUBLISHED HAS BEEN THE
period of the Women's Liberation Movement. Our country
has experienced a radical change of climate. American wom-
en have passed through a revolutionary change of circumstances in personal relations, economic activity, and politics.
They have entered the work force in a mighty tidal wave.
There have been some extremes, probably passing, such as a
tendency to poor grooming and the substitution of "living
together" for marriage, but the greater number of women
have not been diverted from their true objectives by such
matters. They have made great progress against discrimination and inequality with men, and have gone considerable
distance towards attaining equal opportunity with equal pay
for equal work, although still far from reaching these goals.
The Equal Rights Amendment to the Constitution has stalled
just short of ratification by the necessary number of states, but
that battle is not hopeless. Yet there are still mighty barriers

to women exerting their full power and influence in society. There are at this writing two women members of the President's cabinet but only one woman in the Senate. Yet each new year has brought gains.

This has been a decade during which women have loudly voiced their impatience and antagonism to their continuing subordination in the churches in the struggle for their rights. A review of the questions and issues on this point is found in *Women Of Spirit. Female Leadership In The Jewish And Christian Traditions,* by Rosemary Ruether and Eleanor McLaughlin.[1] Women have fought for the modification of the sexist language used in worship and for equal opportunity in theological education and ministry. The struggle for ordination, the focus of the feminist movement in the churches, has been largely won. At least in the major Protestant denominations women can generally be ordained. The Lutheran Church in America and the American Lutheran Church began ordaining women in 1970, and the Lutherans were among the last to capitulate to the women. The Episcopal Church decided to ordain women in 1976, but that action along with the revision of the Prayer Book caused a schism. The issue now is no longer a woman's right to ordination, but rather her equal opportunity for employment as a pastor. She is usually limited to an assistantship or to a small church paying a meager salary. Roman Catholic women have been allowed new minor roles, such as reading lessons at Mass. Sisters have put aside the veil and discarded the traditional garb for contemporary dress, and they have shown tremendous initiative in ministry and service. But the Pope and the bishops continue to deny them ordination and strictly limit their action. Both the Roman Catholic Church and the Protestant Fundamentalist denominations continue to appeal to an interpretation of Scripture which sees a divine order of creation based on "Adam's rib" and an apostolic injunction against women speaking and ministering in the Church as more relevant than the argument based on the New Testament references to

[1] New York: Simon and Schuster, 1979.

women deaconnesses and other ministers. This struggle for parity or at least for greater opportunity in ministry in the homeland churches in recent years appears to have diverted women from seeking the recovery of their former freedom, initiative, and responsibility in the Protestant world mission.

This writer expected the Women's Liberation Movement to spur churchwomen to a determined effort to recover their place of leadership in the Protestant world mission. Unfortunately that desirable achievement has not been realized. The situation remains very much as it was a decade ago. Perhaps it is because Church Women United and the several women's organs of the denominations have substituted ecumenical fellowship for global partnership in mission. Authority in the ruling bodies of the mission boards and societies and administrative power are held almost exclusively by men. Although a woman has become the general secretary of the National Council of Churches, there has been no improvement in its Division of Overseas Ministries. Women have an even smaller place in the power structures of the Evangelical Foreign Mission Association and the Interdenominational Foreign Mission Association. There has been some increase in the number of women members of conciliar denominational boards, and some women have chaired important committees. The governance of the nondenominational societies and the Evangelical denominational boards, except for the few founded by women, is strictly male, and in some instances male domination has strengthened. Out of 620 sending, supporting, and specialized agencies five of the older and larger ones had a woman president or chairwoman for at least part of the decade. Nineteen smaller ones also had women presidents during the 1970s, the majority of them being the founders of their societies. Only two mainline, older sending boards have a woman as the top executive officer, namely, the World Division of the Board of Global Mission of the United Methodist Church and the Church of the Brethren's World Ministries Commission. Sixteen other women are executives of smaller, specialized agencies. Women have continued naturally to direct the several denominational women's societies and auxiliaries, such as the Women's Missionary Union of the Southern Baptist Convention and the Women's Division of Christian Service of the United Methodist Church. There are far fewer women in the second and third level executive posts of the conciliar church boards and in the Division of Overseas Ministries than ten years ago, that is, those persons who administer geographical areas and major functional services. The United Methodists in their World Division have by far the best record since more than thirty-five percent of the executives are women. Women have seldom been admitted to major administrative posts in the nondenominational societies and Evangelical denominational boards, but recently a few women have been appointed candidate or personnel secretaries. However, forty-seven women manage branch offices and field offices of a promotional and financial character generally. None of them involve major policy making.

Little attention has been given the role and status of women in world mission in recent years, excepting some biographies of women missionaries. There is a brief review of the beginnings of women's involvement in Chapter 11 of *Women of Spirit*. A few items on the missionary wife have appeared. Missionary Internship sponsored a Workshop on Woman in Mission in November, 1976.

Dr. Virgil A. Olson, Secretary of World Missions for the Baptist General Conference, read a paper entitled "Understanding Women's Role in Mission Today, An Executive's View," at the Evangelical Foreign Mission Association Annual Conference in March, 1979. It illumines the situation in the agencies which belong to that Association. The paper is based on seventy-six questionnaires returned by women missionaries on furlough and other replies by executives. It reports that restlessness is evident among women and that the role of women in mission is changing. The women express concern about a "subtle, unconcious by-passing of women, especially single women," rather than outright discrimination. Some agencies are no longer appointing many single women. Women candidates are seldom interviewed or counselled by women, and interviewers are usually exclusively male. Wives are not examined as thoroughly as either husbands or single women. While all women under E.F.M.A. agencies are appointed regular missionaries, the wives seldom receive a definite work assignment. Thus, they feel that married women do not receive much recognition. Most denominational boards do not permit wives to work outside the mission, but some interdenominational agencies do so. Educated wives feel that they should have the right to work outside the mission and keep that salary, just as the wife of a pastor in the homeland might do, yet very few boards are giving wives a separate salary check and enrolling them in Social Security. Actual discrimination is felt much more strongly in the field councils than in relations with the home office. Orientation of new missionaries is geared to the men, not women. Many American women feel insecure when control passes through integration from the mission to the national church. Dr. Olson notes that in the Evangelical agencies problems for women are arising in the shift from rural concentration to extensive work in the great urban centers. Challenging ministries for highly educated women are urgently needed. Finally, family counselling for couples and psychological counselling for individuals in field service need to be developed. It is evident from the study that the life and work of the woman missionary is another area in which the Evangelical boards and societies are facing problems which came to the conciliar church boards many years ago.

The old overseas missionary enterprise of the mainline conciliar churches after the end of World War II became an "ecumenical diaconate." Personnel and funds were given to autonomous Third World churches in response to their requests, and the missionaries have "served tables" in the households of sister churches. The boards initiated little new direct work and reduced pioneer evangelization to a minimum. Fewer and fewer missionaries were sent abroad. The nadir was reached about 1978, but now there is once more a slow increase in the missionary staff. Recently, though, some boards are entering creatively into partnership with national churches in pioneer evangelization and church planting. The Evangelical denominational boards and societies maintained and increased their emphasis on the sending of missionaries and have continuously increased their staffs. Consequently the total North American missionary body has grown until in 1976 it numbered 31,186 exclusive of short-term appointees, or almost seventy percent of the world-wide total of Protestant missionaries and more than double the number of a quarter-century earlier.

Statistics of North American overseas missions are reported at intervals of a few years in *Mission Handbook: North American Protestant Ministries Overseas,* edited by Edward R. Dayton.[2] The 1976 edition reported a grand total of 36,950 North American missionaries, of whom 31,186 were regular term persons. Marital status (incomplete) was given as married men 11,702, single men 903, married women 11,375, and unmarried women 4,643. Compare these figures with those of 1950 after World War II and the closing of China, just as personnel was again being built up: married men 3,663, single men 366, married women 3,602, and single women 2,664. All women then made up 60.86 percent of the force. The 1976 percentage was 59.96 percent. Women still continue to make up the majority of North American overseas missionaries, but it is the wives who sustain that majority. Unmarried women are far fewer in terms of percentage than at the height of the women's missionary movement. There are fewer women of single status today than in 1925 when they numbered 4,824 compared with 4,661 married women. There were only 2,664 unmarried women in 1950 after the attrition of World War II and the closing of China, but they grew in strength to 4,828 in 1967. Since then there has been a slight decline in statistics reported: 4,754 in 1970, and now 4,643 in 1976. Actually there are a few hundred more because some agencies did not report persons by marital status.

2 11th edition, Monrovia, Cal.: MARC/World Vision International, 1976.

The tremendous decline of unmarried women in the service of the ecumenical mission boards related to the Division of Overseas Ministries of the National Council of Churches is masked in the total figures for the whole North American enterprise. They formerly were the vast majority of the single women missionaries, but the 691 reported in 1976 are only 14.9 percent of the total of Canadian and U.S.A. unmarried women. The boards and societies related to the Evangelical Foreign Mission Association report 1,028, those connected with the Interdenominational Foreign Mission Association 1,495. There is an overlap in the E.F.M.A. and I.F.M.A. statistics since a few agencies belong to both associations. Unaffiliated agencies reported 1,160. Boards and societies employing more than one hundred single women are: Africa Inland Mission, 120; Assemblies of God, 109; Christian and Missionary Alliance, 155; Evangelical Alliance Mission, 219; Southern Baptist Foreign Mission Board, 312; United Methodist World Division, 142. A few of the nondenominational or Faith Missions have more single women than wives on their rolls, such as the Overseas Missionary Fellowship with 92 to 81 and the Worldwide Evangelization Crusade with 46 to 42. On the whole the Faith Missions allow unmarried women more opportunity in evangelism than do denominational missions.

A new factor in world missions during the past decade is the veritable eruption of very young short-term missionaries. The term "missionary" should not be applied to many of them. The 1976 *Mission Handbook* reported 5,764 or 15.6 percent of the total force, and states that the total number in 1975 may have reached seven thousand. These persons are untrained high school and college youths who go overseas for from a few months to a year or in a few cases as much as two years. They are to be distinguished from these "short termers" who are college graduates and have been employed by mission agencies for two- to four-year terms for many decades. These young people form a kind of Christian "Peace Corps," doing much the same kind of activity as the American government's Peace Corps. They are not reported by sex. Probably half of them are women. They serve as secretaries, English teachers,

teachers of missionaries' children, teachers of classes in religion in English, youth workers, athletic instructors, and construction workers on national church projects. Some agencies, such as the Agape Movement, use them in evangelism. Practically all go on specific project assignments.

Although this book treats Protestant missions, it should be remembered that American Roman Catholic Sisters also serve abroad as missionaries. Their number in 1978 was 2,673, and they represented 180 sending communities and organizations.[3] This is a drastic decline from the high figure of 4,150 in 1968. There has been an important new development for Roman Catholic women in world mission during the last decade, that is, a small number of lay women who are not consecrated Sisters now serve under some agencies.

There is still urgent need for unmarried women in world mission, both in the "ecumenical diaconate" and in pioneer evangelization. It still seems to be true that single women tend to make friends and to identify with nationals more readily than do husbands and wives. They are often more ready to live simply and to adjust to the standard of living of national colleagues.

Renewal and advance in the world mission of the North American Protestant churches awaits the admittance of women to full partnership in the making of policy, strategy, and promotion in the homeland and field councils. It awaits even more laywomen making mission once again their passionate concern. World mission draws its power from voluntaryism, and in the past that has been primarily female voluntaryism.

[3] *Mission Handbook 1978* (Washington, D. C.: United States Catholic Mission Council, 1978).

BIBLIOGRAPHY

SOURCES. The primary sources are the reports — annual or occasional —, magazines, and archives of the individual women's foreign missionary societies and the corresponding general denominational boards. They include also the reports and archives of the Interdenominational Conference of Woman's Boards of Foreign Missions, its successor, the Federation of Woman's Boards of Foreign Missions, the Foreign Missions Conference of North America, its successor, the Division of Foreign Missions (later Division of Overseas Ministries) of the National Council of Churches, and their Committees on Women's Work and Special Program and Funds. Add to these primary sources promotional pamphlets, books on the work, and autobiographies and biographies. Only the more general works used are listed here, and only magazines of the women's boards — none of the general denominational boards — are included in this list. Consult the reference notes, especially those of the first three chapters, for numerous books, periodicals, and other sources not repeated here. No biographies are in the following list, but all those which treat persons mentioned in the text are reported in the notes.

Anderson, Rufus, "Essay on the Marriage of Missionaries," reprinted in *To Advance the Gospel: Selections from the Writings of Rufus Anderson,* ed. R. Pierce Beaver. Grand Rapids: Eerdmans, 1967.

———. *Memorial Volume of the First Fifty Years of the American Board of Commissioners for Foreign Missions.* Boston: the Board, 1860.

Andrews, John A., III, "A.D. Recalls: Betsey Stockton Early Missionary To Hawaii," in *A.D.,* March 1976, p. 30.

Baker, Frances J. *The Story of the Woman's Foreign Missionary Society of the Methodist Episcopal Church, 1869-1895.* Cincinnati: Curts & Jennings; N.Y.: Eaton & Mains, 1898.

Barclay, Wade C. *History of Methodist Missions.* 3 vols. (out of 6). N. Y.: Methodist Church, Board of Missions, 1949-1957.

Beach, Harlan P. *A Geography and Atlas of Protestant Missions,* II. N. Y.: Student Volunteer Movement, 1903; later ed., 1906.

Beach, Harlan P., and Charles H. Fahs. *World Missionary Atlas.* N. Y.: Institute of Social and Religious Research, 1925.

Bennett, Mrs. Fred S., *et al. The Emergence of Interdenominational Organizations among Protestant Church Women.* N. Y.: United Council of Church Women, 1944.

Bliss, Kathleen. *The Service and Status of Women in the Churches.* London: SCM, 1952.

Brown, Arthur J. *One Hundred Years, A History of the Foreign Missionary Work of the Presbyterian Church in the U. S. A.* N. Y.: Revell, 1936.

Calkins, Gladys G. *Follow These Women, Church Women in the Ecumenical Movement.* N. Y.: National Council of Churches of Christ U. S. A., 1961.

Cavert, Inez M. *Women in American Church Life.* N. Y.: Friendship, [1949].

Chamberlain, Mary E. A. (Mrs. W. I.). *Fifty Years in Foreign Fields — China, Japan, India, Arabia. A History of Five Decades of the Woman's Board of Foreign Missions, Reformed Church in America.* N. Y.: the Board, 1925.

Culver, Elsie T. *Women in the World of Religion.* Garden City: Doubleday, 1967.

Daggett, Mrs. L. H., ed. *Historical Sketches of Woman's Missionary Societies in America and England.* New, rev. ed. Boston: publ. by the editor, 1883.

Davis, Grace T. *Neighbors in Christ. Fifty-Eight Years of World Service by the Woman's Board of Missions of the Interior.* Chicago: the Board, 1926.

Davis, Mary A. *History of the Free Baptist Woman's Missionary Society.* Boston: the Society, 1900.

Dayton, Edward R., ed. *Mission Handbook: North American Protestant Ministries Overseas.* 11th ed. Monrovia, Cal.: MARC/World Vision International, 1976.

Dennis, James S. *Centennial Survey of Foreign Missions.* N. Y.: Revell, 1902.

Dennis, James S., Harlan P. Beach, and Charles H. Fahs, *World Atlas of Christian Missions.* N. Y.: Student Volunteer Movement, 1911.

Dickinson, Elmira J. *Historical Sketch of the Christian Woman's Board of Missions.* Compiled in 1897 by Miss E. J. Dickinson, revised and enlarged May, 1905, and Dec., 1907, by Mrs. Helen E. Moses. Indianapolis: the Board, *c.* 1908.

Eddy, Daniel C. *Ministering Women: Heroines of the Missionary Enterprise.* 3rd ed. London: Arthur Hall, Virtue, n. d. (orig. U. S. publication).

Free Baptist Woman's Missionary Society. *The Free Baptist Woman's Missionary Society, 1873-1921.* Providence, R. I.: the Society, 1922.

Gaghee, Frances C. *History and Work of the Woman's Board of Missions of the Cumberland Presbyterian Church.* Evansville: the Board, 1895.

Gracey, Annie Ryder (Mrs. J. T.). *Eminent Missionary Women.* Cincinnati: Curts & Jennings; N. Y.: Eaton & Mains, 1898.

Harford, Mrs. L. R., and Alice E. Bell, *History of the Woman's Missionary Association of the United Brethren in Christ.* Dayton: the Association, 1921. (There is a smaller 1910 book of the same title.)

Harrison, Ida W. *History of the Christian Woman's Board of Missions.* Undoubtedly publ. by the Board, Indianapolis, *c.* 1920.

Heck, Fannie E. S. *In Royal Service. The Mission Work of Southern Baptist Women.* Richmond: Foreign Mission Board, Southern Baptist Convention, 1913; 1927.

Hoskin, Sara Estelle. *Women and Missions in the Methodist Episcopal Church, South.* Nashville: Publ. House, M. E. Church, South, 1923.

Howell, Mabel K. *Women and the Kingdom. Fifty Years of Kingdom Building by Women of the Methodist Episcopal Church, South, 1878-1928.* Nashville: Cokesbury, 1928.

Hunt, Alma. *History of the Woman's Missionary Union.* Nashville: Convention Press, 1964 (Southern Baptist).

Hyatt, Irwin T., Jr. *Our Ordered Lives Confess: Three Nineteenth Century American Missionaries in East Shantung.* Cambridge: Harvard University Press, 1976.

Irwin, Inez H. *Angels and Amazons, A Hundred Years of American Women.* Garden City. Doubleday, Doran, 1934.

Kellersberger, Julia L. *A Life For the Congo: The Story of Althea Brown Edmiston.* N. Y.: Revell, 1947.

Lowrie, Rachel. *The Story of the Jubilee.* West Medford, Mass.: Central Committee for United Study of Missions, 1911.

McAfee, Mrs. L. D. *History of the Woman's Missionary Society in the Colored Methodist Episcopal Church.* Rev. ed. Phenix City, Ala.: Phenix City Herald, 1945.

Miller, Mrs. M. A. *History of the Woman's Foreign Missionary Society of the Methodist Protestant Church.* Pittsburgh: the Society, 1896.

Mission Handbook 1978. Washington, D. C.: U. S. Catholic Mission Council, 1978.

Montgomery, Helen B. *Helen Barrett Montgomery, From Campus to World Citizenship* (edited from her notes and letters by her brother, Storrs Barrett). N. Y.: Revell, 1940. There is no reference to this in notes. See also a pamphlet by Wilhermina C. Livingstone, *Helen Barrett Montgomery.* N. Y. Woman's Amer. Bapt. F.M.S., 1956.

————, ed. *Our Work in the Orient, An Account of the Progress of the Woman's Baptist Foreign Missionary Societies, 1901-1910.* Boston: W.B.F.M.S., 1910.

————. *Western Women in Eastern Lands.* N. Y.: Macmillan, 1910.

Reid, J. M. *Missions and Missionary Society of the Methodist Episcopal Church.* 2 vols. N. Y.: Phillips & Hunt, 1879-1888.

Report of the Ecumenical Missionary Conference, New York, 1900. 2 vols. N. Y.: American Tract Society, 1900.

Ruether, Rosemary, and Eleanor McLaughlin. *Women of Spirit. Female Leadership In The Jewish And Christian Traditions.* N. Y.: Simon & Schuster, 1979.

Safford, Mrs. Henry G. *The Golden Jubilee.* N. Y.: Woman's American Baptist F.M.S., c. 1922.

Steinmetz, Estella H. *Reminiscences, Being a Record of Five and Twenty Years' Progress in the Woman's Home and Foreign Missionary Society of the United Evangelical Church.* Harrisburg, Pa.: United Evangelical Pub. House, 1910.

Stevens, Abel. *The Women of Methodism.* N. Y.: Carleton & Porter, 1866.

Te Winkel, Sarella, *The Sixth Decade of the Woman's Board of Foreign Missions of the Reformed Church in America.* N. Y.: the Board, c. 1935.

Timmons, Sarah L. *Glorious Living, Informal Sketches of Seven Missionaries of the Presbyterian Church in the United States.* Atlanta: Committee on Women's Work, Presbyterian Church U. S., 1937.

Torbet, Robert G. *Venture of Faith.* Philadelphia: Judson, 1955. (History of American Baptist missions.)

Weddell, Sue. *More Than Paper and Ink.* N. Y.: Committee on Christian Literature for Women and Children, c. 1962.

Winsborough, Hollie P. *The Woman's Auxiliary, Presbyterian Church, U. S.* Richmond: Presbyterian Committee of Publication, 1927.

Woman's Board of Missions for the Pacific. *Fifty-five Years, Woman's Board of Missions for the Pacific and Program of Jubilee Meeting.* San Francisco: the Board, 1923.

Woman's Congress of Missions. *Women in Missions: Papers and Addresses presented at the Woman's Congress of Missions, October 2-4, 1893, in the Hall of Columbus, Chicago.* Compiled by Rev. E. M. Whery. N. Y.: American Tract Society, 1894.

Woolover, Eloise A. *Declaring His Glory. Methodist Women at Work around the World.* [Cincinnati: Woman's Division of Christian Service, 1955.]

Worrell, Ruth M. *The Day Thou Gavest, The Story of the World Day of Prayer.* N. Y.: United Church Woman, 1956.

Magazines of Women's Boards

The Evangel, 1918—; from 1881 to 1918 *Woman's Evangel.* W. M. Assn., United Brethren in Christ.

Helping Hand, begun in 1873 as section of *Baptist Missionary Magazine,* later of *The Macedonian,* and eventually incorporated in *Missions.* American Baptist.

Light and Life for Heathen Women, 1869-1872, then *Life and Light for Women,* until 1922, when merged into *Missionary Herald.* Congregationalist.

Mission Gleaner, 1883 until 1917, when merged into *Mission Field.* Reformed Church.

Missionary Annals, 1887-1890. Woman's Presbyterian Board of Foreign Missions of the North West, Chicago.

Missionary Helper, 1878-1919. Free Baptist W.M.S.

The Missionary Link, continuous from 1861. Woman's Union Missionary Society.

The Missionary Messenger, 1930—. Cumberland Presbyterian W.B.M.

Missionary Tidings, 1883 until 1918, when merged into *World Call.* Christian Woman's Board.

Our Mission Fields, 1906-1914; after 1914 *Royal Service.* Southern Baptist.

Woman's Missionary Advocate, 1880-1910. M. E., South.

Woman's Missionary Friend, 1869-1940, named *Heathen Woman's Friend* from 1869 to 1896; merged 1940 into *Methodist Woman.* M. E.

Woman's Missionary Magazine, 1887-1956. United Presbyterian of N. A.

Woman's Missionary Record, 1885-1924. Methodist Protestant.

Woman's Work (uniting *Woman's Work for Woman,* 1871-1885, and *Our Mission Field,* 1886-1889), 1886 until 1924, when merged into *Woman and Missions.* Presbyterian.

INDEXES

I. PERSONS

II. ORGANIZATIONS

Note: There were numerous women's missionary societies that could not be mentioned in a work of this size. They will be found listed in the various Missionary Atlases and Statistical Surveys from Dennis, 1902, to Parker, 1938 *Directory.*

III. PLACES

IV. SUBJECTS